Monetary Implications of the 1992 Process

Monetary Implications of the 1992 Process

Edited by
Heidemarie Sherman, Richard Brown,
Pierre Jacquet and DeAnne Julius

Pinter Publishers
London

© Royal Institute of International Affairs, London;
Institut Français des Relations Internationales, Paris;
Ifo-Institut für Wïrtschaftsforschung, Munich; 1990

First published in Great Britain in 1990 by
Pinter Publishers Limited
25 Floral Street, London WC2E 9DS

British Library Cataloguing in Publication Data

A CIP catalogue record for this book is available from the
British Library

ISBN 0 86187 873 6

Photoset in North Wales by
Derek Doyle & Associates, Mold, Clwyd
Printed and bound in Great Britain by
Biddles Ltd, Guildford and King's Lynn

Contents

Contributors

Christian de Boissieu is a Professor at the University of Paris I (Panthéon-Sorbonne).

Richard Brown studied at the London School of Economics before working at the International Monetary Fund in Washington for five years. On his return to London in 1976 he joined the Bank of England, working in the Economics and International Divisions. He has written a number of articles on international monetary issues and is currently Senior Visiting Fellow at the Institute of European Finance, University of North Wales, Bangor.

Marie-Hélène Duprat is a Research Fellow at the Institut Français des Relations Internationales.

Pierre Jacquet graduated from the Ecole Polytechnique in 1978 and the Ecole Nationale de Ponts et Chaussee in Paris in 1980. After working as a project analyst and consultant on African energy projects with the French development bank, Caisse Centrale de Cooperation Economique from 1979 to 1981, he joined the Institut Français des Relations Internationales (IFRI) where he became associate director in 1985, head of economic studies. He is currently assistant professor of economics at the Ecole Polytechnique and also teaches international economics at the Institut d'Etudes Politiques de Paris.

DeAnne Julius is Chief Economist of Shell International Petroleum Company and was previously Director of Economics at The Royal Institute of International Affairs (Chatham House) in London. She received her Ph.D in economics from the University of California and has worked on taxation and public policy at the World Bank. She is also the author of *Global*

Companies and Public Policy: The Growing Challenge of Foreign Direct Investment, Pinter Publishers for the RIIA, 1990.

Jan Q. Th. Rood is researcher at the Netherlands Institute of International Relations 'Clingendael' in the Hague. His main field of research is international political economy, with special emphasis upon the position of Western Europe in the world economic system.

Heidemarie Sherman is Senior Economist at the Ifo-Institut für Wirtschaftsforschung at Munich. She previously taught at the University of New Hampshire, USA and is the author of a number of papers in German and in English, many of them on the theme of international finance.

Foreword

About twenty years after it first surfaced with the Werner plan and momentarily jumped to the top of European policy-makers' agendas, EMU (European Monetary Union) is once again attracting everyone's attention. In June 1988, the European Council created a committee of central bank governors and experts on monetary questions, the so-called Delors Committee, to propose concrete steps toward the achievement of EMU. The Delors Committee presented its report in May 1989. This was followed in June at the Madrid Summit by the endorsement by European governments of the ultimate goal and proposed first step of the report.

Clearly, there are reasons for such a renewed momentum. European integration has recently acquired an impressive dynamism, largely stemming of course from the 1992 project of completing the European Single Market. Two major forces have pushed the EMU project to the fore. Firstly, the idea was shared by some member states and by the Commission that a monetary union is congenial to the project of a unified market. Secondly, a window of opportunity has been created by the '1992 enthusiasm', which could have a bandwagon effect on monetary integration: since member states appeared so willing to cooperate, why not exploit that goodwill as widely and intensively as possible?

Looking back to the 1970 Werner Report, however, one is struck by the similarities of the approach. A multi-stage process was advocated then, but it soon collapsed, arguably because of disruptive external conditions. Later, the 1978 EMS (European Monetary System) project also envisioned two stages, only the first of which was ever implemented, in March 1979. More generally, there are always good reasons for an ambitious project like EMU to actually stop short of the ultimate objective of monetary unification: indeed, to reach that objective requires a dramatic breach of continuity, while one generally attempts to follow a gradual approach. Gradualism is fine when a centralized decision-making process maintains direction and momentum. However, in a decentralized world of sovereign nations there are many opportunities for reneging on earlier commitments, for both domestic and external reasons. This makes any gradual approach inherently fragile.

Nevertheless, the EMU process has not stood idle for twenty years. The 1970s provided a painful episode of apprenticeship in European monetary cooperation which, after many ups and downs, finally resulted in the major positive step of the EMS. Despite widespread scepticism, the EMS has survived and prospered to the point where most of its earlier detractors have become active supporters. The EMS experience has demonstrated that progress toward monetary union is possible and that that process can yield substantial economic gains for the members. Accordingly, monetary union must be thought of as an ongoing process rather than an ultimate goal. Each step in the right direction brings Europe closer to that goal, and each time such a step is possible, an interesting question is how far it will take the participants along the path toward the ultimate goal.

When our three institutes, the Ifo-Institut für Wirtschaftsforschung in Munich, the Royal Institute of International Affairs (Chatham House) in London, and the Institut Français des Relations Internationales (IFRI) in Paris planned their contribution to the 1989 project of the Tokyo Club Foundation for Global Studies,[1] they decided to conduct joint research related to the EMU process. It had to be recognized, however, that an abundant literature has shed light on many aspects of EMU, and that the field was already crowded with many publications. None the less, we decided that we could bring useful insights by focusing on the present characteristics of monetary policy-making in major European countries. This book includes the resulting papers on central banking in Germany, France and the United Kingdom written for the Tokyo Club.[2] It also benefits from an additional country study on the Netherlands, prepared by Jan Rood of the Netherlands Institute of International Relations, The Hague.

The rationale of our approach is simple: in order to get a good grasp both of the incentives and of the difficulties involved in the EMU process, and therefore indirectly to tackle the question of the prospects for its evolution, it is necessary to concentrate on the present situation, the institutional setting in the member countries, and the objectives – explicit or implicit – that shape both monetary policy-making and the national stance toward EMU. It requires focusing on historical developments and factual analysis, rather than indulging in speculation over possible future institutional arrangements. Of paramount concern is how current institutional and political factors help in understanding the management of monetary policies in Europe and are likely to shape the path of future European monetary integration.

This study focuses on four EMS countries, although EMU is best conceived of as a common adventure for all EC countries. We believe that the case studies selected cover a wide range of positions with respect to European monetary cooperation, and that they allow us to highlight the major issues involved although, of course, the political and institutional conditions are unique to each country. Germany provides undisputed leadership within EMS. France is one of the most active supporters of EMU. The UK is not a full EMS member, since it does not participate in the exchange rate mechanism. Finally, the Netherlands provides an interesting case of a country that is already closely tracking German monetary policy.

The four country studies of national monetary policies provided an input to an overview paper, written at Chatham House by James Morsink. That paper in turn served as a basis for the editors in preparing the introductory and concluding chapters for this book.

The introduction (Chapter 1) highlights the major issues involved with monetary union, and their relationship with the creation of the Single Market. Chapters 2 to 5 are devoted to the country studies themselves. The conclusion (Chapter 6) presents the editors' views on the process of monetary integration in Europe.

The editors, November, 1989

Notes

1. The Tokyo Club Foundation for Global Studies, or 'Tokyo Club', was created by the Nomura Securities Co., Ltd. in 1987. Its aim is to address by scholarly research problems of global interest and make the findings available to the international public. The five associated research institutions are The Brookings Institution (United States), The Ifo-Institut für Wirtschaftsforschung

(Germany), The Institut Français des Relations Internationales (IFRI, France), The Royal Institute of International Affairs (Chatham House, United Kingdom) and The Nomura Research Institute (Japan).
2   These papers were also published in the *Tokyo Club Papers* No. 3, Tokyo Club Foundation for Global Studies, Tokyo, 1989. The authors wish to thank the Tokyo Club participants as well as outside commentators for useful comments on earlier versions of these papers during the Tokyo Club July and October 1989 discussion sessions.

1   Economic and monetary integration in the EC

Monetary and economic union

In this chapter we first consider conceptual issues which arise in the relationship between monetary and economic union. We then go on to review the process of economic integration in the EC before analysing some of the implications of the 1992 process for monetary union.

In its pure form, a monetary union may be defined as a set of countries using a single currency. At a minimum it would require that any national currencies be fully convertible and exchange rates irrevocably fixed. In effect there would be a single currency, although several nominally different currencies may coexist, as in the Belgium–Luxembourg Economic Union (BLEU). Irrevocably fixed exchange rates either require that national central banks be placed under a single monetary authority or that the separate monetary authorities be obliged to subordinate national economic policies to the goal of exchange rate stability. If different central banks were to pursue mutually inconsistent monetary policies, then exchange rates would eventually have to be changed. Even if the different central banks were to pursue mutually consistent monetary policies, the existence of more than one monetary authority, which implies the possibility (however remote) of a change in exchange rates, means that self-fulfilling speculative runs on central banks could not be excluded.[1]

Certain observers see monetary union as an integral part of the project to complete the internal market in the EC (the 1992 process). Indeed, at the Hanover Summit of the EC in June 1988 the leaders of the EC recalled that 'in adopting the Single

European Act, the member states of the Community confirmed the objective of progressive realization of economic and monetary union'. However, it is important to distinguish between a monetary union and a common market, which is sometimes referred to as an economic union. A common market entails the free movement of goods, services, and factors of production.[2] The ideal common market is one in which nationality labels on products, persons, or capital have no economic significance. A common market (or, for that matter, a free-trade area) is neither a necessary nor a sufficient condition for a monetary union. Barriers to trade may exist within a monetary union, such as the West African Monetary Union (WAMU),[3] and conversely currencies in a free-trade area may float against each other, as in the United States–Canada Free Trade Agreement.

A monetary union changes the nature of the constraints on its members' fiscal policies. There are conflicting views about the

Figure 1.1 Budget deficits of the EC countries

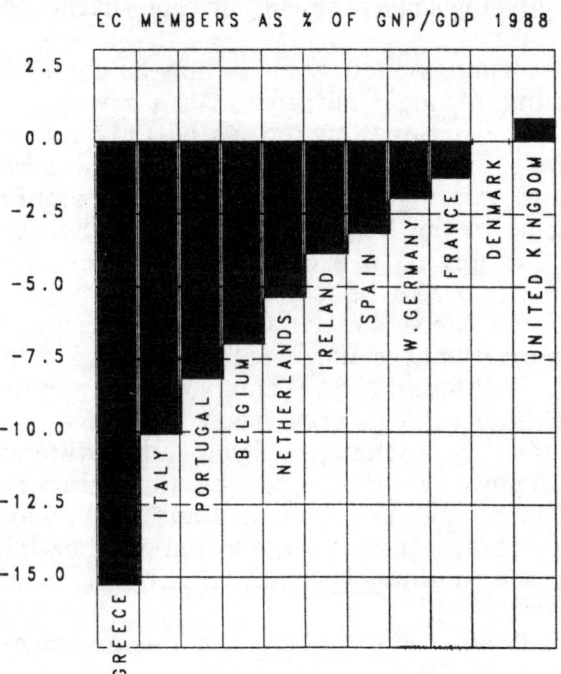

SOURCE: OECD, EC.

degree of fiscal coordination it requires. There may be fairly wide limits within which fiscal policy can move without having an effect on the ability to maintain fixed exchange rates. For example, in Canada the individual provinces are allowed to run substantial deficits: several provinces have deficits in excess of 10 per cent of revenues and Saskatchewan runs a deficit of almost 30 per cent of revenues. But clearly overly lax fiscal policies will eventually have overwhelming consequences on interest rates. While many governments in the EC are committed to policies of deficit reduction, according to comparable figures from the Organization for Economic Cooperation and Development, budget deficits[4] in EC countries range from 15.3 per cent of Gross Domestic Product (GDP) in Greece and 10.1 per cent in Italy, through 2 per cent in Germany and 1.3 per cent in France, to budget balance in Denmark and a budget surplus in Britain (see Figure 1.1).

Economic integration in the EC

The EC was established by the Treaty of Rome, which was signed on 25 March 1957 and came into effect on 1 January 1958. The Treaty prescribed the creation of a common market within a 'transitional period' of twelve years. However, actual progress towards economic integration, although impressive, fell short of the full requirements of the Treaty. With the publication of a white paper in 1985 the Commission of the EC launched an initiative to complete the common market by the end of 1992. This initiative is commonly known as the 1992 process. The aim of achieving a common market was included in the Single European Act (SEA),[5] in a formulation stronger than that in the Treaty of Rome.

The concept of economic integration is clear in theory, but the degree of progress towards it is hard to measure in practice. If there existed centralized, competitive markets for all goods, services, and factors of production (distinguished by location and time of availability), it would be a simple task to compare prices and infer the progress towards integration from the reduction in the dispersion in prices. Indeed, we shall use this approach when we consider the integration of capital markets. However, the heterogeneity of most goods and services, and certainly of labour, precludes the possibility of such markets. So we are forced to consider other measures of integration, including the extent of legal impediments and the size of product and factor flows.

With respect to manufactured goods, as most tariffs and quantitative restrictions were dismantled between 1958 and 1968, trade within the EC as a share of total trade and as a share of Gross Domestic Product (GDP) grew rapidly until about 1972 and then levelled off. Jacquemin and Sapir (1988) use the ratio of intra-EC imports to total imports (i.e. intra- and extra-EC imports) to analyze the evolution of intra-EC trade in manufactured goods for the first ten EC countries (EC-10). From 1958 until 1972 the share of intra-EC imports increased steadily, reaching a peak of 61 per cent. The ratio remained at about 60–61 per cent between 1973 and 1979, declined in 1980, and has since levelled off at about 58 per cent. Following a period of rapid growth until 1973, intra-EC-12 imports and exports in France and Germany registered a slight relative decline. Since 1972, only the new member countries have seen major increases in intra-EC trade. Britain witnessed a dramatic rise in intra-EC imports and exports in 1973–4 and these indices are now at similar levels to those in France and Germany (see Figures 1.2 and 1.3).

Figure 1.2 Intra-EC(12) imports as a percentage of total

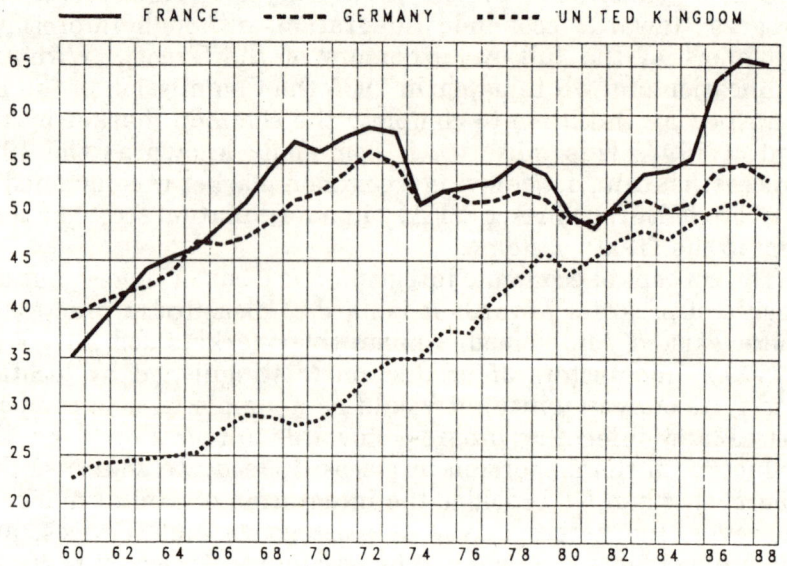

Figure 1.3 Intra-EC(12) exports as a percentage of total

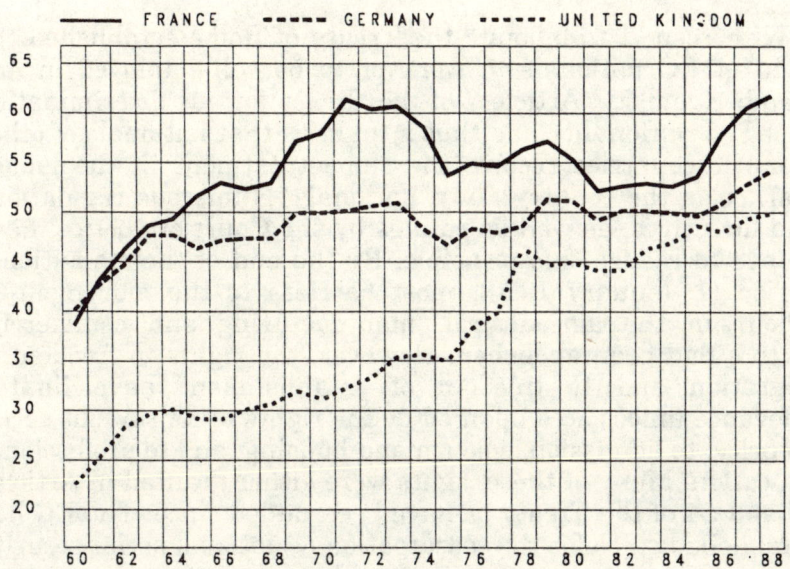

The 1992 process contains several provisions which should increase intra-EC flows of goods and services. The Commission plans to make significant progress in opening up competition for government-procured goods. Under the SEA, the passing of legislation in this field comes under the qualified majority voting rule, which means that a single country can no longer block acceptance. Similarly, future directives for technical standards can now be adopted by qualified majority vote. The application of the principle of mutual recognition and the capacity to establish EC standards are gradually dismantling technical barriers. Recently, certain barriers to trade in transport and financial services have been removed, and further liberalization is expected. In insurance and banking, the right of establishment in other member countries has been secured and progress is being made in legislating minimum harmonization requirements. Road haulage and shipping are being liberalized, and progress in civil aviation is expected. In the area of indirect tax harmonization and fiscal frontiers, the white paper seeks an approximation of value-added and excise tax rates, with a view to suppressing fiscal obstacles at intra-EC frontiers. However, the elimination of barriers to trade in agriculture, steel, textiles and fisheries is hardly mentioned in the white paper, and existing restraints will prevent further integration in these areas.

With respect to labour,[6] the Treaty of Rome established the right of EC nationals to work or to be self-employed in any member country. Article 7 of the Treaty forbids discrimination based on nationality and thus stipulates that nationals of other member countries receive the same treatment in the labour market as the country's own nationals. Numerous regulations and directives, as well as rulings by the Court of Justice, have helped to realize this principle. By the end of the transitional period (1 January 1970), most barriers to the movement of labour in the agricultural, manufacturing and commercial sectors had been abolished. However, the rights to freedom of migration and to freedom of establishment have limited relevance unless accompanied by the rights to continuous social security; to admission, sojourn and housing; and to professional education. Many of these rights were either granted in Articles 48 and 54 of the Treaty or have been added since. The EC has established rules for the coordination of national social security systems, which cover all the major branches of social security: sickness, old age and unemployment.

Despite the gradual elimination of legal barriers to migration and substantial differences in wage rates among member countries, intra-EC labour migration has been modest. Using data on the stock of migrants, Straubhaar (1988) shows that changes in intra-EC migration were dominated by changes in extra-EC migration (see Figure 1.4). The total number of workers who had migrated from one of the original six EC countries (EC-6) into another increased from about 500,000 before 1960 to about 830,000 in 1968, remained almost constant until the beginning of the 1980s, and then decreased to about 650,000. Between two-thirds and three-quarters of intra-EC migrants consisted of Italians. Whereas Italian emigration was spread over the entire EC-6, the remaining intra-EC migrants stayed close to home: workers from Benelux moved particularly within Benelux, and French (German) migrants preferred areas in Germany (France) and in Benelux near the national border. The number of intra-EC-6 migrants changed much less dramatically than the number of migrants from outside the EC-6. The intra-EC-6 share of the total migrants working in the EC-6 decreased from 44 per cent in 1958 to 32 per cent in 1968, decreased further to about 20 per cent in 1974, and has remained constant since then.

Figure 1.4 Stock of migrants in the EC

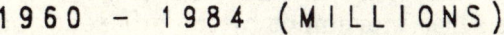

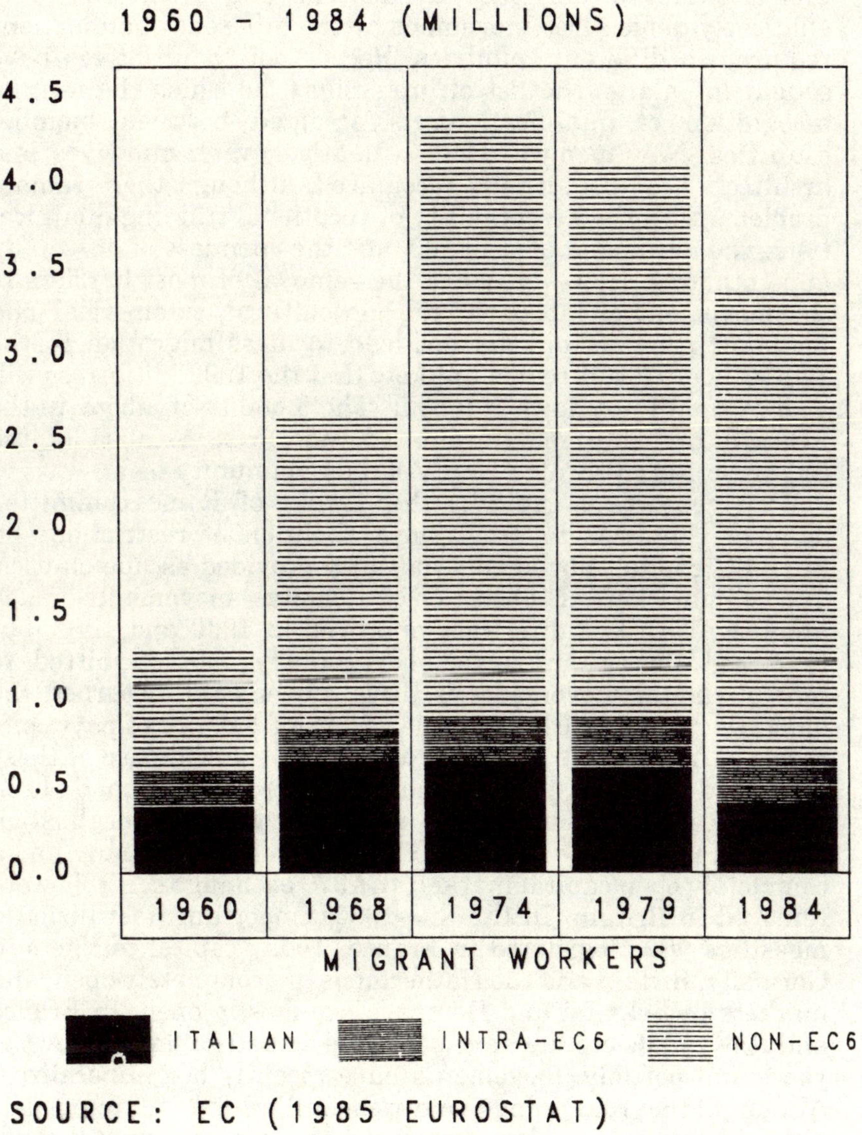
1960 – 1984 (MILLIONS)
4.5
4.0
3.5
3.0
2.5
2.0
1.5
1.0
0.5
0.0
1960
1968
1974
1979
1984
MIGRANT WORKERS
ITALIAN
INTRA-EC6
NON-EC6
SOURCE: EC (1985 EUROSTAT)

The 1992 process will reduce the remaining barriers to the movement of skilled labour in the EC. Until recently professional workers, such as dentists and architects, were effectively denied free movement by the different qualifications required in different countries. Recent policy initiatives have sought to enlarge the list of professions for which the mutual recognition of qualifications is accepted between member countries. Now medical doctors, dentists, vets, midwives and architects are all mutually recognized, although there remain problems with the acceptability of vocational training qualifications, the movement of students, and the openness of university appointments. However, since the removal of most barriers to the movement of labour in the agricultural, commercial and manufacturing sectors did not lead to mass migration in the 1960s and 1970s, it seems unlikely that the 1992 initiatives will lead to significant flows of labour. The mobility of labour in the EC will probably remain limited, not least because of the linguistic and cultural diversity of the Community.

With respect to capital,[7] the Treaty of Rome committed member countries to progressive abolition of restrictions on intra-EC capital movements, but also provided escape clauses. The elimination of obstacles to capital movements made progress, with two directives approved in 1960 and 1962, but regressed thereafter. A member country was permitted to control capital movements if these movements disturbed the domestic capital market (Article 73) or for balance of payments reasons (Article 109). Several countries made wide use of these safeguard clauses to re-establish controls that had been removed earlier. Considerable progress towards liberalization has been made since the late 1970s, when only Germany had a completely open capital market. In 1979 exchange controls were removed in Britain. In the mid-1980s important liberalization measures were legislated in France. Today capital markets in Germany, Britain and the Netherlands are completely open, and markets in Belgium and Denmark are mostly open. In France and Italy, trade credits have been free of restrictions for several years and portfolio movements have recently been liberalized. Although the remaining countries still retain an important array of controls, evidence on interest rates and capital flows suggests that capital markets in Europe are becoming increasingly integrated. Interest rates on domestic markets have shown a tendency to converge and to move together (see Figure 1.5). In addition, the differentials between domestic and

Figure 1.5 Money-market interest rates

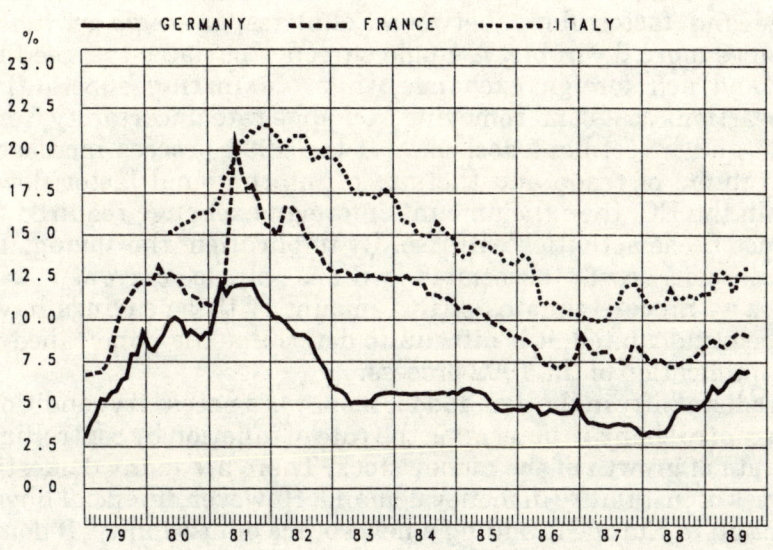

SOURCE: DEUTSCHE BUNDESBANK, OECD.

Euromarket rates have narrowed.

The 1992 process will further increase the integration of capital markets in the EC. The white paper recommends action by the EC in four main areas: directives to remove obstacles to capital movements, regulatory requirements to ensure the stability and efficiency of capital markets, tax harmonization measures to remove fiscal distortions, and borrowing and lending activity conducted directly by EC institutions. In June 1988, the EC Council of Ministers adopted a timetable for the removal of remaining controls on capital movements. France and Italy are to lift restrictions on short-term flows by 1 July 1990, while Spain, Ireland, Greece and Portugal will follow suit by the end of 1992.[8] Also by the end of 1992, Belgium will cease to operate its dual exchange market.

Monetary implications of the 1992 process

The 1992 process may increase the benefits of a single currency in the EC, complicate national monetary control, and threaten the viability of the EMS as it now stands. We examine each of these issues in turn.

To the extent that further economic integration increases trade and factor flows between countries, a *single currency* becomes more desirable. A single currency obviates the need to buy and sell foreign exchange, thus eliminating substantial transactions costs and removing exchange rate uncertainty from trade and investment decisions. If the 1992 process increases the volume of trade and the size of international factor flows within the EC, then the amount of foreign exchange required to finance these activities will rise. By implication, the savings in transactions costs associated with a single currency will increase. Since estimates of the amount of these savings have not been calculated, it is difficult to determine the importance of this implication of the 1992 process.

Predictability in the demand for money is a necessary condition for a central bank to determine the rate of inflation by controlling the rate of growth of the money stock. There are many domestic sources of instability in money demand. However, financial liberalization in Europe is adding a new source of instability. If domestic residents hold only the domestic currency, then a country's money demand may be identified with the domestic demand for the country's currency. On the other hand, if firms and individuals hold diversified portfolios, a phenomenon known as currency substitution, a country's money demand and the demand for the country's currency are different. The currency composition of cash balances may change even if the demand for money remains unchanged. It follows that even if there is a stable demand for money in, for example, Britain the demand for sterling may not be stable. Hence, control of the rate of growth of the stock of sterling is not sufficient to determine the inflation rate in Britain. Indeed, demand for sterling depends on economic conditions elsewhere, which makes monetary control more difficult.

The 1992 process will affect both the transactions and speculative demands for diversified portfolios, thus complicating monetary control. As increased economic integration works to create a single market in the EC, the incentive for firms and individuals to hold transactions balances in more than one EC currency will increase. Further, in some countries the removal of capital controls will allow firms and individuals to hold diversified portfolios for speculative purposes, i.e. to diversify risk and for other reasons related to financial management. However, currency substitution is already an important phenomenon. As we noted earlier, trade in goods and services within the EC is significant, and both Germany and Britain have had open capital markets for more than a decade. Hence, as the monetary authorities in both countries (but especially Britain) have discovered during the 1980s, monetary control is already problematic.

In theory, the liberalization of capital movements may threaten the viability of the European Monetary System (EMS). Over the past decade, differences in inflation rates and economic performance between the countries participating in the exchange rate mechanism (ERM) of the EMS made periodic changes in the bilateral central rates necessary (see Table 1.1). In the early years of the EMS these realignments usually involved a discrete jump in the price of one or more currencies,[9] and therefore gave rise to large profit opportunities. Before a discrete change in an exchange rate, traders in the foreign exchange market were presented with a one-way speculative option: they stood to make huge gains if they sold the weak currency just before the change and bought it back at a lower price just afterwards. It was precisely this sort of one-way speculative option that eventually brought about the demise of the Bretton Woods system in the early 1970s.

Table 1.1 Realignments in the European Monetary System 1979–89

	German mark	French franc	Italian lira	Dutch guilder	Belgian franc	Danish crown	Irish punt
24 Sept. 1979	+2					−3	
30 Nov. 1979						−5	
22 Mar. 1981			−6				
4 Oct. 1981	+5.5	−3	−3	+5.5			
21 Feb. 1982					−8.5	−3	
12 Jun. 1982	+4.25	−5.75	−2.75	+4.25			
21 Mar. 1983	+5.5	−2.5	−2.5	+3.5	+1.5	+2.5	−3.5
22 July 1985	+2	+2	−6	+2	+2	+2	+2
6 Apr. 1986	+3	−3		+3	+1	+1	
4 Aug. 1986							−8
12 Jan. 1987	+3			+3	+2		

Source: Deutsche Bundesbank

Capital controls played a significant role in preventing or minimizing these speculative flows. By making it illegal for domestic residents to hold foreign currency and for foreigners to hold domestic currency, capital controls in France insulated the domestic money market from the Euro-currency market. The effectiveness of these controls can be seen by comparing the short-term interest rate in the domestic market with that in the Euro-currency market (see Figure 1.6). In the Euro-currency market the short-term interest rate rose sharply when a devaluation was expected, while the domestic rate did not change dramatically. The movement in the Euro-currency market is fully consistent with the expectations about currency realignment: if the devaluation is expected to be 5 per cent within one month, interest rate differentials on one-month deposits should be 60 per cent (5 per cent × 12) per annum to compensate for the expected capital loss. Capital controls helped to prevent these pressures from being transmitted to the domestic money market.

Figure 1.6 Short-term interest rates: France

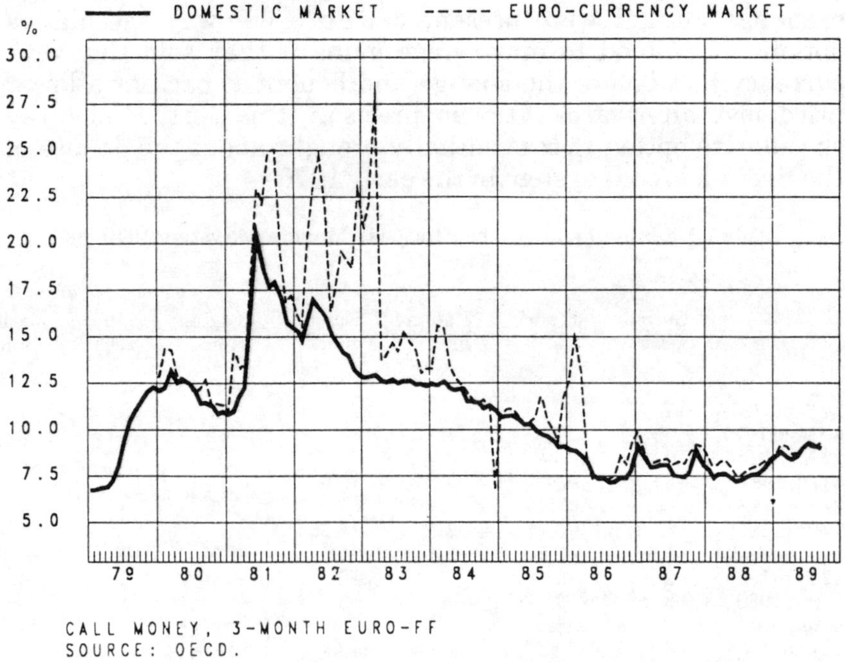

CALL MONEY, 3-MONTH EURO-FF
SOURCE: OECD.

In the absence of capital controls, anticipations of discrete jumps in exchange rates will lead to massive speculative attacks on central banks. As long as the resources of central banks are finite, a fixed exchange rate cannot be defended indefinitely. This raises the possibility that in a crisis the exchange commitment will be abandoned, which is equivalent to a collapse of the system of fixed exchange rates. However, the convergence in inflation rates since 1983 and the improved management of realignments suggests that such speculative crises may be avoided. Since 1983, there has been only one discrete jump in the French franc–Deutschmark exchange rate (in April 1986: see Figure 1.7). Indeed, if sufficient economic convergence is achieved, there is no need for nominal exchange rate changes. If this is not the case, realignments will be needed. If they are sufficiently frequent so that the change in the central rate is less than the width of the band (which is twice the margin, i.e. 4.5 per cent), then a discrete jump in the nominal exchange rate may be avoided.

Figure 1.7 Exchange rate of the French franc against the Deutschmark

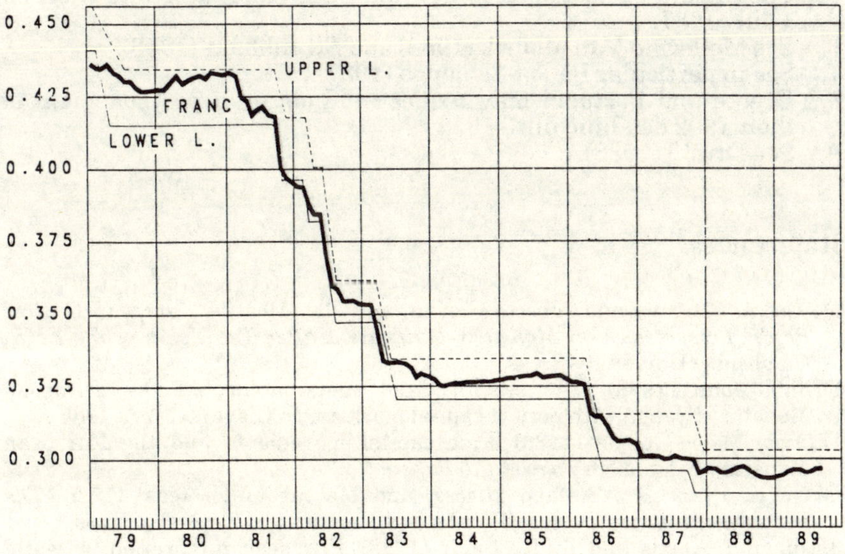

SOURCE: DEUTSCHE BUNDESBANK.

In summary, the 1992 process has revived the dynamics of monetary integration, and increased the potential benefits from monetary union. It also reduces, to some extent, the costs of EMU by increasing factor mobility. However, it will not, by itself, bring about monetary union. Currency substitution and its implications for national monetary control are already important phenomena. Finally, the EMS could survive long beyond 1992 provided that its members are prepared to accept

German monetary leadership or carry out realignments in a timely fashion. However, these alternatives may raise political difficulties.

Notes

1. See Obstfeld (1988).
2. By contrast, a customs union or a free-trade area simply entails the free movement of goods and services.
3. The WAMU consists of Benin, Burkina Faso, Ivory Coast, Mali, Niger, Senegal and Togo. The common currency is the CFA franc, which is issued by the Banque Centrale des Etats de l'Afrique de l'Ouest (BCEAO).
4. The definition combines central and local government spending.
5. The SEA was enacted on 17 February 1986 and came into effect on 1 July 1987.
6. See Molle and Van Mourik (1988) and Straubhaar (1988).
7. See in particular Padoa-Schioppa (1987).
8. Greece and Portugal may request and obtain a postponement of their 1992 deadline until 1995.
9. See Driffill (1988).

References

De Cecco, Marcello and Alberto Giovannini (eds) (1989) *A European Central Bank? Perspectives on Monetary Unification after Ten Years of the EMS*, Cambridge University Press.

Driffill, John (1988) 'The stability and sustainability of the European Monetary System with perfect capital markets,' in Giavazzi *et al*. (1988).

Duprat, Marie-Helene (1988) 'Free capital movements and the European Monetary System,' in *Tokyo Club Papers No.2*.

Giavazzi, Francesco, Stefano Micossi and Marcus Miller (eds) (1988) *The European Monetary System*, Cambridge: Cambridge University Press.

Jacquemin, Alexis and Andre Sapir (1988) 'European integration or world integration?', *Weltwirtschaftliches Archiv*, 124:1, 127–39.

Krugman, Paul (1979) 'A model of balance-of-payments crises', *Journal of Money, Credit, and Banking*, 11: 311–25.

McDonald, Frank and George Zis (1989) 'The European Monetary System: towards 1992 and beyond', *Journal of Common Market Studies*, 27:3 (March): 183–202.

Molle, Willem and Aad Van Mourik (1988) 'International movement of labour under conditions of economic integration: the case of Western Europe', *Journal of Common Market Studies*, 26:3 (March): 317–42.

Obstfeld, Maurice (1988) 'Competitiveness, realignment, and speculation: the role of financial markets', in Giavazzi et al. (1988).

Padoia-Schioppa, Tommaso (1987) *Efficiency, Stability, and Equity*, Oxford: Oxford University Press.

Robson, Peter (1987) *The Economics of International Integration*, 3rd ed, London: Allen and Unwin.

Straubhaar, Thomas (1988) 'International labour migration within a common market: some aspects of the EC experience', *Journal of Common Market Studies*, 27:1 (September): 45–62.

Tokyo Club Foundation for Global Studies (1988) *Tokyo Club Papers No.2.*

2 Central banking in Germany and the process of European monetary integration

Heidemarie C. Sherman

Introduction

The completion of the internal market by 1992 is another important step toward economic and monetary union as agreed by the heads of government of the European Community at their 1969 meeting in the Hague. As the ground for this new initiative for a barrier-free common market was prepared by the success of the European Monetary System in promoting a convergence of the member economies, so the 1992 programme gives new impetus for growing monetary integration, the ultimate goal of which is a currency union with a European central bank and a common currency.

In order better to understand the German position on future monetary integration in Western Europe, it is necessary to throw some light on the history of central banking in Germany, on the particular experience of this country during a century which saw two world wars and two great periods of inflation, destroying the country and wiping out people's wealth twice in one lifetime.

The German central bank

History

In its present form, as the *Deutsche Bundesbank*, the German central bank only dates back to 1957, when the Bundesbank Act concluded the post-Second World War reorganization process, begun in 1948, of the German banking system by converting the *Bank deutscher Länder* into the *Deutsche Bundesbank*.

The first German central bank, the *Reichsbank*, had been created in 1875 after the unification of the German states into the *Deutsches Reich* in 1871. Like the Prussian Bank of 1857, from which it emerged, it had private shareholders, but a board of trustees consisting of civil servants. There was a distinct provision, however, which was to keep the Bank independent from the fiscal administration. The 'Bank Law' of 1875 provided for a large measure of state supervision and control, giving the *Reich's* Chancellor responsibility for the entire bank administration and the right to instruct the board of directors and the branches. By law the board of directors was quite autonomous, members being appointed for life. In order to guarantee the independence of the Bank from the Treasury, any business with fiscal administration of the Reich or with the federal *Länder* was to be reported to the Bank's 'central committee', which then decided whether or not such business was appropriate (Borchardt, 1976, p. 16).

With the outbreak of the First World War, a number of laws became effective, creating the institutional environment in which hyperinflation could materialize. One of the most important laws concerned the abolition of the gold convertibility of the currency, which meant not only that Germany *de facto* adopted flexible exchange rates, but also that there were no longer any quantitative constraints on money creation by the central bank. The institutional arrangement by which the *Reich's* Chancellor headed the central bank would have prevented any independent non-accommodative monetary policy. But given the sentiment of the time, the central bank management in any case saw its prime task as to supply the government with the required monetary means. Even when, after the war, the Autonomy Law of 1922 put responsibility for the central bank exclusively into the hands of the board of directors, there was little change in the close relationship between the Bank and the government.

As a result of financing the war with a large volume of short-term debt and a huge increase in the money supply, the rate of inflation began to rise. This was less noticeable in the exchange rate than in the domestic purchasing power. At the end of the war the mark had lost less than half of its foreign exchange value, whereas the price index of industrial finished products had risen to 477 by October 1918 (July 1914 = 100). Although some taxes had been raised in 1916, these served mainly to service the rapidly rising debt. The inflation which accompanied the war was not only a German phenomenon, but occurred in all the warring countries, regardless of whether a higher or lower proportion of the war had been financed via taxes. But while France and England succeeded in controlling inflation after the war, in Germany it exploded into hyperinflation. Explanations include the high and rising budget deficits (despite the fiscal reform of 1919–20), war reparations, especially in the form of goods, and finally the monetary policy of the *Reichsbank*. Until the Autonomy Law was passed in 1922, the Bank had no choice but to accept the full volume of Treasury bills. And the credit expansion begun by the now autonomous Bank in the summer of 1922 was economically sound, as it served to overcome a serious credit crunch and to prevent mass unemployment which the new Weimar Republic would not have survived politically. The Bank's discount policy, however, did contribute to the inflation process. By keeping the discount rate far below the rate of inflation (in July 1922 it was still at 5 per cent), the Bank facilitated the replacement of reparations goods and the reconstruction of production facilities, but it also failed to restrain private investment to an economically reasonable volume. Hyperinflation started in January 1923, when the central bank credit to the government exploded. Domestic purchasing power and the exchange rate plummeted. During January 1923 alone the exchange rate fell from RM 7,260 to the dollar to RM 49,000. After successful stabilization of the exchange rate at RM 20,000 until the end of May, the free fall started with the final flight from the mark. In November one dollar was worth RM 4,200 billion. The financial and monetary systems broke down completely; the economy disintegrated.

It is the hyperinflation of 1923, leading to the chaotic conditions of Germany's monetary system and her economy, to the destruction of the monetary assets of the middle class, to shattering strain in the social structure caused not only by the massive redistribution of wealth from creditors to debtors, which has ingrained itself so deeply in German memories. It was not least the fear of another inflation that was responsible for the failure to introduce, in the following years, an active countercyclical economic policy to fight mass unemployment. The political upheaval witnessed in the decade following the great inflation also had its origin to a large extent in the various consequences of the inflation (Pfleiderer, 1976, p. 199).

The new Bank Law of 30 August 1924 reorganized the existing *Reichsbank*. In stark contrast to the Bank Law of 1875, article 1 of the new law clearly determined the independence of the *Reichsbank* from the government. The *Reichsbank's* board of directors managed the bank and determined its foreign exchange, discount, and credit policies. Loans to the government were limited to a maximum of RM 100 million for no longer than three months. Another RM 200 million credit could be granted to the national postal and railroad systems. Besides the general meeting representing the share owners, there was a general council consisting of fourteen members, seven of whom were German; the other seven had to be foreign nationals. One of the German members was president of the board of directors and chairman of the general council.

The revision of the Bank Law on 27 October 1933 abolished the general council and thus the influence of foreigners. The president and the members of the board of directors were henceforth appointed and dismissed by Hitler. The rule that the bank should only discount good commercial bills was now interpreted very generously, and credit was extended freely by way of 'work procurement bills' and later 'special bills'. Parallel to the subjugation of the central bank to the interests of the regime, control of public finances was wrested from parliament, giving the government power over the budget and public debt. Finally, the Deutsche Reichsbank Law of 16 June 1939 subjected the bank to the 'unrestricted sovereignty of the *Reich*', making it directly responsible to the *Führer*.

The monetary and fiscal policies under Hitler, characterized especially by practically unlimited money creation and war financing, once again led to the destruction of the German currency.

The creation of the modern German central banking system

The currency reform of 20 June 1948, containing the currency law, the issuance law, and the change-over law, laid the foundation for the postwar monetary system in its present form. In the area comprising the Federal Republic and West Berlin, the *Reichsmark* was replaced by the *Deutsche Mark*.

The Reichsbank was liquidated and a two-stage central bank system was established, largely patterned on the US Federal Reserve System. Land central banks had existed since early 1947 in the American and the French occupation sectors; in the British sector they were founded on 1 March 1948, together with the *Bank deutscher Länder* (Law No. 60 of the US Military Government). To achieve uniformity of the legal bases of the various land central banks as well as conformity with that of the

Bank deutscher Länder, the laws establishing the land central banks were replaced with identical laws of the military governments, becoming effective on 15 April, 1949 (Law No. 66 of the US Military Government). The land central banks functioned as legally independent central banks in their respective territories. The *Bank deutscher Länder*, their common affiliate, was responsible for issuing the paper currency, for policy coordination, and for certain central tasks, including capital controls. The top organ of this two-stage central bank system was the central bank council, consisting of its president, the presidents of the land central banks, and the president of the board of directors of the *Bank deutscher Länder*. The central bank council was responsible for the discount rate and the newly introduced minimum reserve policy. It also determined the directives for open market policy and credit creation (see Spindler et al., 1957, p. 11ff.).

From its inception the *Bank deutscher Länder* was independent of any German political authorities, including the Federal Government which began operating in September 1949. In 1951 it achieved full autonomy from the Allies. Given the bad experiences with a central bank subject to the instructions of the government (the old *Reichsbank* before 1924 and the new *Reichsbank* from 1933 on), which twice had led to the total destruction of the currency, the principle of an independent central bank after the war was never questioned.

Article 88 of the German basic law which became effective in 1949 prescribed the creation of the *Bundesbank* as the central bank of the Federal Republic. The Deutsche Bundesbank Act of 26 July 1957 abolished the two-stage central bank system and instead established the *Deutsche Bundesbank*. It emerged from the merger of the land central banks with the *Bank deutscher Länder*. The land central banks, losing their legal independence, became part of the Bundesbank as major regional administrative entities (Deutsche Bundesbank, 1989).

The institutional structure of the Bundesbank

The Bundesbank, which is located in Frankfurt for as long as Berlin is not the capital of the Federal Republic, has equity capital of DM 290 million, which belongs to the Federal Government. Any profits in excess of legal reserves must be turned over to the Federal Government. This does not, however, give the government any rights which would impinge on the Bundesbank's policy autonomy.

The organizational structure consists of the Central Bank Council, the Directorate, and the presidents of the land central banks. The positions of the Central Bank Council and the Directorate are equivalent to that of federal ministries. At the top of the organization is the Central Bank Council, the policy-making body of the Bundesbank, consisting of the president and the vice-president of the Bundesbank, the other members of the Directorate, and the presidents of the eleven land central banks. It is chaired by the president and in his absence by the vice-president of the Bundesbank. The Central Bank Council meets every two weeks and makes decisions based on simple majority vote. It determines monetary and credit policy, as well as the directives for the management and administration of the Bank

The Directorate is the central executive organ, responsible for carrying out the decisions of the Council. It carries out the central bank's business

- with the Federal Government;
- with those banks which are responsible for central tasks all over the Federal Republic;
- in the foreign exchange market and transactions with foreign countries;
- in the open market.

The Directorate consists of the president, the vice-president and up to eight (at present five) additional members. Members of the Directorate must have outstanding professional qualifications. They are nominated by the Federal Government and – after hearings before the Central Bank Council – are confirmed by the president of the Federal Republic for terms of not more than eight and not less than two years.

The land central banks are the major administrative offices of the Bundesbank in the federal *Länder*, including West Berlin. The land central banks are responsible for transactions with their particular land, the public administrations within the land and the banks in their district. They also supervise the branch offices (currently around 200) which the Bundesbank maintains in all bigger towns. The land central banks are headed by an executive board, consisting of the president, the vice-president, and – in the case of the bigger institutions – one other person. The presidents, who by law are at the same time members of the Central Bank Council, are appointed in a similar manner as the members of the Directorate. They are, however, nominated by the Bundesrat, the upper house of parliament, which is bound by the recommendation of the respective land government. This way the Federal Government is unable to dominate the composition of the Central Bank Council. The vice-presidents are appointed by the president of the Bundesbank on the recommendation of the Central Bank Council in which they have no vote, however. The land central banks have advisory boards consisting of representatives of the banks, business and labour. Their function is to provide the contact between the Bundesbank on the one hand and banks and business on the other. Via the land central banks the different economic conditions in the various *Länder* enter into Bundesbank considerations.

Primary responsibilities of the Bundesbank and its relationship to the Federal Government

Section 3 of the Bundesbank Act defines the duties of the Bundesbank: to regulate the currency in circulation and the supply of credit with the goal of 'safeguarding the currency', and to provide for the smooth functioning of payments transactions within the domestic economy and with foreign countries (Spindler et al., 1957, p. 105).

The stability of the currency, in the sense of maintaining its domestic purchasing power as well as its purchasing power in terms of foreign currencies, does not only depend on monetary and credit conditions, but on various other factors especially economic policy, fiscal policy and wage and social policies. The Federal Government is responsible for these other policy areas, including matters concerning the exchange rate. Only the area of monetary and credit policy is the responsibility of the Bundesbank. When, besides the traditional task of a central bank to maintain an orderly monetary system, the Bundesbank Act emphasizes the responsibility of the Bundesbank for the stability of the currency, this does not mean that price stability, insulated from the overall economic picture, can be the only goal of monetary policy. But, by law, it has always been considered its primary goal. The Bundesbank Act does not only make the Bundesbank independent of any government directives; it explicitly specifies that the basic obligation of the Bundesbank to support the general economic policy of the Federal Government must not conflict with the primary task of monetary policy (Section 12).

While the Bundesbank Act contains no rules for the case of serious disagreement and tensions between the government and the Bundesbank, Section 13 does contain rules which foster cooperation and mutual consultation. Thus the Bundesbank is obliged to advise the Federal Government on monetary policy matters of substantial importance and to furnish it information upon request. The Federal Government is obliged to invite the president of the Bundesbank to its discussions of matters concerning monetary and exchange rate policy. Likewise, members of the Federal Government have the right to attend meetings of the Central Bank Council, where they have no vote but may propose motions. They may also request to have a decision deferred for up to two weeks. The same kind of procedure applies to the attendance of the Bundesbank at discussions of the Financial Planning Council.

Besides the Deutsche Bundesbank Act, the main statutory bases of monetary policy are the 1967 Economic Stability and Growth Act and the 1961 External Trade and Payments Act. The basic provisions on the supervision of the banking system are to be found in the Banking Act, which became effective in 1962.

Instruments of monetary policy

The Bundesbank has a wide variety of instruments at its disposal with which it can influence interest rates and liquidity conditions in the money market. Unlike other countries, the instruments of German monetary policy are limited to those which leave the financial sector largely to the free play of market forces. Thus the Bundesbank cannot limit the amount of credit granted to non-banks or determine administratively the interest rates in credit or bond markets. Instead the Bundesbank tries to influence indirectly the behaviour of banks as suppliers of credit and that of households and business as demanders of credit via changes in interest rates and bank liquidity.

The major interest rate instruments are changes of the discount and the Lombard rates as well as changes in the interest rates on open-market operations with repurchase agreement.

The major liquidity instruments include changes in the minimum reserve requirement. In addition, the Bundesbank can set quantitative and qualitative limits on the banks' access to discount and Lombard credit, can enrich bank liquidity by moving public-sector deposits into the banking system, and can add or drain liquidity by open-market purchases or sales of money-market paper or foreign exchange.

The flexible control of the money market (via open-market operations with repurchase agreement in commercial bills and securities, exchange rate swaps and repurchase operations as well as the sale of short-term Treasury bills and shifts of Federal Government deposits into the banking system) has only been practised since 1979 and has been refined since then. It must be considered quite successful.[1]

Monetary and exchange rate policies in theory and practice

Monetary and exchange rate policy may be divided into two periods, which are defined by the exchange rate regime. Until 1973, i.e. until the final demise of the Bretton Woods System, fixed exchange rates had to be maintained, a duty which had important consequences for the operation of monetary policy, frequently leading to conflicts between internal and external balance. With the introduction of the system of flexible exchange rates in March 1973, monetary policy received a long-awaited degree of freedom, as foreign economic influences lost their dominance. Of course, the Bundesbank's obligation to intervene in the foreign exchange market was not fully cancelled. Thus an intervention duty existed until 1979 within the European Currency Union (the so-called 'snake')[2] and has existed since then within the European Monetary System (EMS). Certain obligations have also resulted from international coordination efforts (e.g. the Louvre Accord of February 1987), which have included the stabilization of exchange rates.

Monetary policy under fixed exchange rates

During this early period, which was dominated by Keynesian economic thought, German monetary policy was employed as a countercyclical policy instrument, although price stability was its central concern, as laid down in the Bundesbank Act.

Main operating targets Until 1973 the German monetary authorities sought to attain their policy objectives by acting on interest rates on bank lending and deposits and by controlling 'bank liquidity', i.e. the 'free liquid reserves' of the banking system. 'Free liquid reserves' consist of liquid assets which can readily be converted into central bank balances. They comprise excess reserves on deposit with the Bundesbank, domestic money market paper, money market investment abroad[3]), unused rediscount margins (quotas) and, as a negative item, short-term Bundesbank advances against collateral (Lombard credit). The latter component was deducted because this type of central bank credit could not be drawn on automatically and had to be repaid within a short period. This German liquidity concept differs from other definitions of bank liquidity by excluding required reserves and including secondary reserves. It is a measure of the potential lending capacity of the banks rather than a measure of their current reserve position (OECD, 1973, pp. 39–40).

For purposes of analysis the determinants of free liquid reserves are divided into those arising predominantly from market forces and those arising predominantly from credit policy. The major market forces are: changes in the currency in circulation; changes in the net foreign exchange reserves of the Bundesbank and in the foreign money-market investments of the banks; changes in the net balances of non-banks (particularly public authorities) with the Bundesbank; and changes in the public authorities' money-market indebtedness to the banking system (including the Bundesbank). The task of the policy instruments was to offset or reinforce the impact of market forces in order to bring about the level of bank liquidity considered to be consistent with the desired trend in bank lending. To this end the Bundesbank employed the following policy instruments: changes in minimum reserve requirements, changes in rediscount quotas, and open market operations. Open market operations in money-market paper were generally conducted with the banks, and while changing the composition of bank liquidity did not change its total supply. On the other hand, open market operations with non-banks and operations in government bonds, which were conducted at certain times, did affect bank liquidity.

The free liquid reserves permitted the banks to meet by themselves the extra demand for central bank balances originating with the expansion of bank assets and liabilities. For two decades, the banks' behaviour was such that they tried to keep a minimum of free liquid reserves at all times, so whenever these reserves shrank to a minimum, the banks reduced new lending in order to prevent a further decline in liquid reserves.

When the banks' behaviour changed in 1971–2, the Bundesbank decided to eliminate free liquid reserves almost totally.

Monetary policy under external constraints The 1950s were the decade of the German 'economic miracle', a period characterized by high rates of growth, full employment, surpluses in the government's budgets, and surpluses in the current account of the balance of payments. Following the currency reform of June 1948, however, the Federal Republic had started out as a deficit country. But as early as 1951 the picture changed. Until 1954 the surpluses did not pose a problem and did not conflict with the price stability policy of the central bank. They did become a problem during the period from 1955 to 1957, initiating the first postwar public discussion about the conflict between the requirements for internal and external balance and a possible revaluation of the Deutschmark (Emminger, 1976, pp. 487–8).

The problems for German monetary policy became really serious with the introduction of currency convertibility at the end of 1958. Until then there had been three periods of restrictive monetary policy: 1948, 1950–1 and 1955–6. During these three early episodes German monetary policy had not been hampered too much by foreign influences because of the lack of convertibility. The central bank had other difficulties, however. In the mid-1950s boom, when the central bank introduced countercyclical restrictive policies, it was severely attacked by Chancellor Adenauer and representatives of industry for trying to abort the upswing. In addition, there was the problem of controlling the money creation process with the monetary instruments at hand. The contractionary effects of minimum reserve and open-market policies were more than offset by the large volume of bills presented for discounting. As a result, the banks' money creation capacity did not slow down until the second half of 1956, when the boom had already lasted one year (Dürr, 1973, p. 85).

The worldwide economic slowdown from summer 1957 to spring 1959, underpinned by a successful fight against inflation in several deficit countries, as well as the devaluation of the French franc, helped to reduce foreign demand and restore a current account situation which was no longer in conflict with an inflation-free expansion of domestic demand. Domestic price stability, which had increasingly been at risk since mid-1955, was regained. The cost of living stabilized, or even declined, supported by a steep drop in world market prices, following the end of the Suez crisis. This permitted the Bundesbank to continue its expansionary policy. Interest rates were lowered several times until in January 1959 the discount rate was cut to 2.75 per cent, its lowest level ever. Bond rates also declined from 8 per cent in mid-1957 to a low of 5.2 per cent in April 1959. The decline in German interest rates promoted heavy short-term as well as long-term capital outflow, solving – at least temporarily – the German balance of payments problem. This successful achievement of the three macroeconomic goals, full employment, price stability, and balance of payments equilibrium – was crowned at the end of 1958 with the return of the Deutschmark (and several other European currencies) to full convertibility. For Germany, which had abolished almost all capital controls in the preceding years, this was only a formal confirmation of *de facto* achievements.

The decade of the 1960s was a period of considerable growth and employment, interrupted by a slowdown in 1963 and the first postwar recession, in 1967. Although, compared to later periods, prices in the 1960s can be considered to have been rather stable, the rate of inflation increased from one growth cycle to the next. Intractable current account surpluses resulting from an undervalued currency led to imported inflation. In addition, wage increases reflecting serious labour shortages contributed to 'home-made' inflation.

The Bundesbank's attempt, in autumn 1959, to introduce a tighter policy to slow down the new boom was swamped by a massive capital inflow. The resulting increase in the money supply could only be compensated in April 1960. The revaluation of the Deutschmark in early 1961 was too late and too small, failing not only to break the boom but also to make monetary policy effective again. The Bundesbank had to pursue a policy of low interest rates until 1965, a policy which would have been appropriate in a recession, but not in a period of excessive employment and rising prices.

The recession of 1966–7 was partly due to the absence of an effective countercyclical policy for seven years. Instead of slowing down the demand expansion early on to make it conform to the real production possibilities, which were limited especially by the diminishing growth rate of the labour force, the fixed exchange rate prevented a contractionary monetary policy until the time at which 'accommodating' domestic inflation together with anti-inflationary measures abroad had resulted in a current account deficit. By then the long-lasting boom had created a lopsided output structure in favour of capital goods, which was geared to a strong investment demand which could not last for ever. Thus when the belated price-stabilizing monetary policy became effective and when the public authorities cut back their investment expenditure, the economy succumbed to a pronounced recession.

It had become quite obvious that monetary policy was severely constrained by the balance of payments and could no longer play the dominant role in overall economic policy. With the Economic Growth and Stability Act of 1967 the government intended to provide additional policy instruments. In conjunction with other measures, expansionary monetary policy helped to bring about the cyclical turnaround. But in the upswing the conflict between domestic price stability policy and mounting foreign exchange inflows resumed. The revaluation of the Deutschmark by 9.3 per cent in the fall of 1969, inducing an outflow of speculative funds, would have permitted a restrictive monetary policy. But the Bundesbank did not take advantage of this opportunity, presumably because it wanted the new administration to introduce contractionary fiscal measures (Dürr, 1973, p. 87). Not until March 1970 did it raise the discount rate from 6 to 7.5 per cent and the Lombard rate from 9 to 9.5 per cent. By then domestic inflationary pressures had become well entrenched. The revaluation had been delayed too long by domestic political fighting to prevent the economy from overheating. Inflationary pressures emanated especially from the explosion of wages which had started in September 1969. Unit wage costs in industry surged by more than 13 per cent in 1970, compared to increases of 6 per cent in the United States and 9 per cent for the average of the major European countries. Despite the revaluation, inflation continued, reaching and at times even exceeding foreign levels. Not until 1973, following the transition to floating exchange rates, was Germany able to disassociate itself from the generally prevailing inflation trend, returning to the lower end of the international inflation range.

But in the preceding inflationary phase the Bundesbank was powerless. As early as the middle of 1970, however, it was forced to ease monetary policy again, not least in response to the sharp decline in American interest rates, bringing the discount rate back to 5 per cent and the Lombard rate to 6.5 per cent by April 1971. But the interest rate differential had nevertheless shifted in favour of Germany, leading to massive capital flow from the United States to Germany, forcing the closure of the German foreign exchange market and the freeing of the Deutschmark exchange rate in May 1971. From January 1970 to May 1971 there had been net capital inflows of DM 35.3 billion on top of a current account surplus of DM 5.6 billion. Although restrictive measures of the Bundesbank (increase in minimum reserves, cyclical surtax) withdrew DM 24 billion from the economy, the money supply M2 exceeded its year earlier level by 17 per cent in May 1971. Foreign money markets were said to have not only assumed the role of the German banks as suppliers of credit, but also to have become an 'ersatz central bank' (Emminger, 1970).

The period since 1973

The freedom from having to intervene in favour of the US dollar created an important prerequisite for an effective monetary policy. The decision to let the currency float against the dollar was taken on 19 March 1973 by the Federal Government in conjunction with the other countries then participating in the snake. With the exception of the United Kingdom, Ireland and Italy, the EC countries as well as Sweden and Norway agreed to let their currencies float as a block against the dollar.

Another important prerequisite for an effective monetary policy was created when the Bundesbank eliminated the free liquid reserves of the banks. Even before the speculative wave of February/March 1973, the Bundesbank had started to reduce bank liquidity. Then, in order to absorb the liquidity resulting from the heavy capital inflows in February and March, the Bundesbank raised the minimum reserve ratio and reduced the allowable volume of rediscounts to 60 per cent of the quota. Together with the almost 100 per cent reserve requirement on the banks' foreign liabilities, these measures shrank the banks' free liquid reserves to almost zero; since then the Bundesbank has prevented the build-up of such reserves.

Upon eliminating the free liquid reserves, the Bundesbank started to control directly the creation of central bank money. Fine-tuning the central bank money stock required new techniques. In April 1973 the Bundesbank for the first time bought bills in the open market under the agreement to repurchase them after ten days. The difference between the purchase and sales price was geared to market interest rates – then running to between 11 and 16 per cent. In this initial period, these interest rates fluctuated widely, reaching 20 per cent for several days in April and July and once even 40 per cent.

To reduce these fluctuations, the Bundesbank offered the banks special Lombard credit – then at 13 per cent – which could be called the very next day by simply cancelling the granting of special Lombard credit. On the other hand, in order to absorb any excess central bank balances of the banks, the Bundesbank offered Treasury bills with maturities of 5 to 10 days at rates in the neighbourhood of the discount rate.

Major operating targets In the 1970s the Bundesbank increasingly shifted its policy focus to the control of the quantity of money. The decision to change its monetary policy concept was taken not only in response to the rising influence of monetarism, but also in response to the dramatically accelerating inflation resulting from the first oil price shock. The embittered fights between the unions and industry, but also between the private and the public sectors, for a larger share of a shrinking pie reduced the tolerance for a counterinflationary monetary policy and instead endogenised higher rates of inflation in everyone's expectations. This was reflected by the rush into real estate, by double-digit wage increases, and by an excessive expansion of government expenditure. Of course, the Bundesbank's limited room for manoeuvre, constrained by fixed exchange rates prior to 1973, played an important role in this. The Bundesbank's initial efforts to cut back the rate of monetary growth following the transition to flexible exchange rates was not accepted by society and therefore led to a recession. So it seemed necessary to increase the transparency of future financial conditions and rates of inflation and thereby to influence the behaviour of the market participants in the direction of a consensus on price stability.

The quantitative control of the money supply according to the monetarist school seemed interesting to the Bundesbank because its central tenets agreed with the Bundesbank Act and with the convictions of the German central bankers: In the medium term, inflation is a monetary phenomenon; therefore the responsibility for price stability rests with the monetary authorities which can control the money supply (Schlesinger, 1988, p. 5).

The Bundesbank chose the central bank money stock as the target variable. The central bank money stock (CBMS) comprises currency in circulation and the required minimum reserves for domestic liabilities. The required minimum reserves are calculated at the constant reserve requirement of January 1974 in order to exclude the influence of changes in minimum reserve requirements. They thus represent at unchanged weights all sight deposits, time and savings deposits (with maturities of less than four years) at domestic banks. The weights are 16.6 per cent for sight deposits, 12.4 per cent for time deposits, and 8.1 per cent for savings deposits. The different types of deposit are thus represented in the minimum reserve component of the CBMS in a ratio of 4:3:2, roughly corresponding to their degree of liquidity. The CBMS thus differs from the conventional definitions of the money supply by not comprising the total stock of liquid liabilities at banks, but only the fraction depending on the particular reserve requirements. In contrast, currency in circulation enters the CBMS with its full weight.

Since the central bank money stock describes changes in bank deposits only indirectly via the adjusted required reserves, it is not contained in the consolidated balance sheet of the banking system, but must be calculated from the balance sheet of the Bundesbank. By comprising those liabilities of the Bundesbank which – like currency in circulation – are either part of the money supply from the start or – like the minimum reserves on domestic liabilities – derive from the banks' monetary expansion, the CBMS reflects money creation by the central bank as well as the banks. It thus mirrors in the central bank balance sheet the money stock held by all economic agents. Calculated at actual reserve requirements, it also represents the central bank's contribution to money creation. If the central bank did not provide additional central bank money to the banks to support currency in circulation and the maintenance of growing minimum reserves, the banks' money creation process would soon come to a standstill. One of the advantages of the CBMS is that it underlines this final responsibility of the central bank.

Another advantage is purely statistical. Because the monthly CBMS is calculated from average stocks (daily in the case of currency, qualifying days of four banking weeks in the case of the required reserves), it is not subject to the randomness of end of the month statistics like those for M1 or M2. In addition, because of their source, CBMS data are also available sooner.

A disadvantage, especially in public discussions, has been the fact that the CBMS is easily confused with the 'monetary base', a concept well known from the monetarism debate. In fact, the statistical differences are minor, consisting primarily in the inclusion of minimum reserves against foreign liabilities as well as bank's excess reserves in the monetary base. More serious are the differences in interpretation. According to the monetarists, the monetary base gives the primary policy stimulus, initiating the process of monetary expansion; the academic monetarists also consider the monetary base a variable which is directly controllable by the central bank. The CBMS, as defined by the Bundesbank, is a broadly defined weighted money supply concept; it is considered an intermediate target variable, which the Bundesbank can influence via control of money market conditions.

The CBMS was the official target variable until the end of 1987, when the Bundesbank switched to M3 as the money supply to be targeted from 1988 on. Like CBMS, M3 is a broadly defined money stock, largely covering the same monetary components. M3 comprises currency in circulation as well as sight deposits, time deposits with a maturity of less than four years, and regular savings deposits. The big difference is that CBMS represents these domestic bank liabilities by the minimum reserves held against them, calculated at constant 1974 reserve requirements. Thus currency in circulation has a much greater weight in CBMS than in M3. At times when currency in circulation is the fastest-growing money supply component, CBMS will overstate the actual rate of monetary expansion. In addition, over time the actual structure of minimum reserves has changed significantly from that in 1974, which is the basis of the definition of CBMS and the weighting of its components. But because of the similarity of their components, CBMS and M3 have exhibited a largely parallel movement during the past ten to fifteen years. Both monetary aggregates have been shown to be positively related, in a rather stable way, to the growth of the nominal productive potential and negatively to the change in interest rates. The existence of such stable relationships facilitates the medium-term orientation of monetary policy in deriving the annual monetary target, the assessment of the current evolution of the money supply, and the required dosage of corrective policy measures. Furthermore, econometric studies have shown that changes in the money stock (CBMS or M3) tend to precede changes in expenditure, implying that the central bank's control of the money stock can influence the trend of nominal GNP and of the general price level (Deutsche Bundesbank, 1985).

Monetary targeting The Bundesbank adopted and published a monetary target for the first time in December 1974. It has held on to this practice ever since, although the money supply target has been formulated in different ways (see Table 2.1). The Bundesbank has always derived the monetary target for a given year from its ideas about the desirable pace of economic activity during that year. The targets have been based on economic forecasts arrived by consensus with the government and normative settings of the major variables. The focus has been on the average annual growth rate of the productive potential and the desired rate of inflation. Over the medium term the money supply control by the Bundesbank has thus revealed the bank's intention to provide for steady growth.

Table 2.1 Monetary targets and actual outcomes %

| Year | Target: Growth of central bank money stock or M3* | | | Actual outcome (rounded figures) | | |
	Q4 to Q4	annual average	more precise	Q4 to Q4	annual average	target achieved
1975	around 8	–	–	10	–	no
1976	–	8	–	–	9	no
1977	–	8	–	–	9	no
1978	–	8	–	–	11	no
1979	6–9	–	lower end	6	–	yes
1980	5–8	–	lower end	5	–	yes
1981	14–7	–	lower half	4	–	yes
1982	4–7	–	upper half	6	–	yes
1983	4–7	–	upper half	7	–	yes
1984	4–6	–		5	–	yes
1985	3–5	–		5	–	yes
1986	3½–5½	–		8	–	no
1987	3–6	–		8	–	no
1988	3–6	–		7	–	no
1989	around 5	–				

*From 1988: money supply M3.

Source: Deutsche Bundesbank.

Under normal circumstances the medium-term growth of the money demand corresponds to that of the real productive potential. An expansion of the money supply equal to the growth of the productive potential thus provides sufficient scope for the financing of expenditure growth. Because expenditures, the productive potential as well as the money supply, are nominal variables, their growth must be derived at current prices. Until 1984 the Bundesbank used the 'unavoidable price increase' in the derivation of its monetary target. In this way it took account of the fact that price increases which have already entered the decisions of the economic actors may be reduced only gradually. The rate of inflation which was tolerated did, however, always fall short of the actual rate or that forecasted for the year to come. Once price stability had largely been achieved at the end of 1984, the concept of the 'unavoidable price increase' was suspended. After ten years of setting monetary targets, which in each year had been based on too high a rate of inflation, the 1985 target, providing for a higher utilization of productive resources at stable prices, closely approximated the concept of monetary policy geared to the growth potential (Deutsche Bundesbank, 1989, p. 100).

From 1979 to 1988 the monetary target was defined as a range (see Table 2.1). This was to permit the Bundesbank on the one hand to account for various technical problems of measuring and controlling the monetary expansion. On the other hand it allowed for extra room for manoeuvre to respond to internal or external disruption without having to abandon the idea of medium-term control. An important consideration in using target ranges and in the question of how stringently monetary targets have to be met was the behaviour of exchange rates and their consequences for the domestic economy. Since 1973 exchange rates have fluctuated greatly. Real exchange rates can and must shift drastically if structural disequilibria in the balances of payments are to be corrected. A monetary policy which gives priority to exchange rate stabilization along purchasing-power-parity lines rather than being primarily directed at domestic requirements is not a universally accepted alternative today. It would neither do justice to the different causes of exchange rate fluctuations, nor would it take account of the remarkable differences which still exist between the economic goals of the major industrialized countries, Schlesinger, 1988, p. 9. The Bundesbank has always maintained, however, that monetary policy must, from case to case, take exchange rate developments into consideration, especially when repercussions of massive exchange market disruptions on domestic economic policy must be feared (Dudler, 1984, p. 56ff.).

Monetary policy experience since 1973 The external component of the money supply has been a disturbing factor for German monetary policy even after the introduction of flexible exchange rates. Obligations assumed as a party to the European Currency Union (the 'snake') and the European Monetary System (EMS) have frequently prevented the pursuit of the appropriate monetary targets (cf. Table 2.1). Because of its increasing importance as an international reserve currency, the Deutschmark soon became the preferred substitute whenever speculation turned against the dollar. In order to prevent the exchange rate from breaching the upper limit of the band in the European currency arrangements, the Bundesbank has had to intervene in favour of the dollar.

The large degree of international openness of the German economy, its high export dependence, has brought with it the belief that monetary policy must take into consideration any 'undesirable' exchange rate effects. In such cases the monetary authorities may be willing to reduce the potential fluctuation of the exchange rate on a more or less informal basis – like the Louvre Accord – and thereby constrain its scope for monetary policy action.

By entering into international exchange rate agreements, by assuming formal or informal intervention duties, the Bundesbank, like any other participating central bank, 'voluntarily' gives up a measure of autonomy. When autonomy is not surrendered, i.e. when the central bank tries to sterilize the effects of intervention on the domestic money supply, the exchange rate stabilization efforts lead only to a different composition of the portfolios of the central bank and the private sector. Under the realistic assumption that domestic and foreign money-market instruments are close substitutes, the effect on exchange rates will be minimal.

Although the period 1973–5 saw the first oil price crisis, excessively high wage agreements and a recession, the Bundesbank's policy was not constrained by international considerations. It initially took advantage of the newly gained degree of policy freedom to fight the high rate of inflation. When these restrictive measures and a cyclical decline abroad led to an economic slowdown, the Bundesbank changed to an expansionary course. Although domestic interest rates declined more than those abroad and although (the domestic component of) the money supply increased considerably in 1974 and 1975, relatively greater price stability prevented the Deutschmark from downside pressure. But from 1975 to 1978 the monetary targets – which many considered to be too high anyway – were consistently exceeded for exchange rate reasons. In 1976 in particular, the Bundesbank intervened heavily in favour of the other currencies in the snake. In 1977 and 1978 intervention was primarily carried out in favour of the dollar. During these two years the increase in the DM/$ rate, in the central bank money stock and its foreign component closely paralleled each other.

Beginning in 1979 the Bundesbank changed course. But the sharp policy tightening during the following two years, which contributed to the recession of 1981–2, occurred in response to external factors. The coincidence of 'home-made' inflation with the second oil price crisis, the deficits in the current account and the strengthening of the dollar in early 1981 were the factors which, via a depreciation of the Deutschmark, were believed to lead to a cumulative inflationary process and to an undesirable devaluation of the Deutschmark in the EMS. Therefore, in 1980, the Deutschmark was heavily supported by unsterilized intervention against the dollar as well as against the EMS currencies. In 1981, however, the very restrictive monetary policy of the Bundesbank necessitated interventions in favour of the other EMS currencies, while the Deutschmark still needed support against the dollar.

When in the summer of 1982 a decline in the rate of inflation and a surplus in the current account emerged, the Bundesbank switched to an expansionary policy stance. The monetary target threatened to be exceeded again in the spring of 1983 when tensions in the EMS caused massive capital inflows, leading to very rapid growth in the central bank money stock. As a result of the currency realignment in March, the capital flows reversed and interest rates rose, permitting the Bundesbank to meet its monetary target by year-end.

From early 1983 to the spring of 1985 money supply growth was retarded by the steep rise of the dollar. While the weakness of the Deutschmark provided a welcome stimulus for German exports, it also threatened domestic price stability. The Bundesbank therefore intervened heavily in support of the DM/$ exchange rate. Despite a large increase in the domestic component of the money supply, the expansion of the central bank money stock slowed from 8 per cent in the first quarter of 1983 to 4 per cent in the second quarter of 1985.

The dollar peaked in February 1985 at almost DM 3.50. Its decline was accompanied in the EMS only by the Italian lira (and sterling), whose devaluation was confirmed by the currency realignment of 22 July. The Bundesbank lowered its interest rates and raised the rediscount quota of the banks. The devaluation of the dollar, which was promoted by the Plaza Agreement of September, led to increasing tensions in the EMS, only temporarily resolved by the realignment in early April 1986. The interventions within the EMS and the Bundesbank's policy of lowering interest rates in concert with foreign central banks led to an acceleration of money supply growth.

From 1986 to 1988 the Bundesbank tolerated monetary expansion in excess of the target in order to meet its obligations under the Louvre Accord. Exchange rate considerations were allowed to take precedence because the drastic decline of oil prices and of the dollar held down the domestic cost of living. When the monetary authorities tried to rein in the money supply in 1987, the stock market crash forced them to reverse policy. It was not until mid-1988 that the Bundesbank seriously began to tighten its policy. By then the ground had been prepared by the US central bank, which had adopted a restrictive stance at the beginning of the year. Between June 1988 and October 1989, the German discount rate was raised from 2.5 to 6 per cent and the Lombard rate was similarly raised in several steps to 8 per cent.

German monetary policy and the EMS As long as the Bundesbank's decisions to let foreign exchange considerations influence its monetary policy are voluntary, one might argue that policy autonomy is not endangered. In principle this also applies to the European Monetary System, which – in contrast to the Bretton Woods System – is not an agreement among governments, but simply one among central banks. Thus, on principle, the Bundesbank could leave the EMS at any time without the approval of the government. This legalistic view is unrealistic, however, as it totally neglects the political dimension. The political obligations, which the Bundesbank assumed by becoming a member of the EMS and by emphasizing its willingness to support the evolution of the system, are extremely strong. And as long as the Bundesbank is a member of the EMS, the system's legal requirements and consequent economic constraints are also binding on the Bundesbank. As a result, the decision-making processes of German monetary policy have become more difficult, although – aside from considerable temporary disturbances – the Bundesbank's room for manoeuvre has never been seriously constrained. After all, it is the Deutschmark which has become the anchor of the EMS.

That the Deutschmark has become the centre or anchor currency is no accident. It is the natural consequence of the Bundesbank's monetary policy which has consistently achieved relatively greater price stability. Policy convergence in other EMS countries, especially France, has reduced the frequency of currency realignments and drawn the EMS closer together. To be sure, the stabilization of exchange rates has necessitated a growing volume of intervention (see Table 2.2). The liquidity effects of these foreign exchange purchases have frequently posed serious problems for the Bundesbank. Since the finance ministers repeatedly failed to agree – or failed to agree in time – on a realignment of exchange rates, the Bundesbank was not always able to sterilize these effects. In addition to the expansionary monetary impact of interventions in the foreign exchange market, the EMS has had important direct effects on German monetary policy. Thus in January 1987, under the pressure of a flood of capital pouring into Germany from the other EMS countries, the Bundesbank finally gave up its resistance to further interest rate cuts. This was the price at which the finance ministers agreed to a small exchange rate correction. And despite excessive monetary growth, interest rates were cut again in November of the same year, because the finance ministers refused to relieve the newly arisen tensions by another realignment.

With these measures the German Bundesbank wants to contribute to a stabilization of the DM-exchange rate vis-a-vis the US dollar as well as vis-a-vis the EMS currencies and reduce the tensions in the financial markets.... Together with the interest-rate changes in the other EC countries, this underlines the intention to strengthen the exchange-rate structure in the EMS and to continue acting in accordance with the Louvre Accord. (Deutsche Bundesbank 1987.)

In 1988, too, the Bundesbank was more concerned with avoiding tensions in the EMS than with expanding the money supply in

Table 2.2 Deutschmark interventions in the EMS*
(billion DM)

Calendar year	Mandatory	Intra-marginal	Total	Effect on German liquidity
1979†				
Purchases	–	– 2.7	– 2.7	– 2.4
Sales	+ 3.6	+ 8.1	+11.7	+11.7
Balance	+ 3.6	+ 5.4	+ 9.0	+ 9.2
1980				
Purchases	– 5.9	– 5.9	–11.8	–11.1
Sales	–	+ 1.0	+ 1.0	+ 0.6
Balance	– 5.9	– 4.9	–10.8	–10.5
1981				
Purchases	– 2.3	– 8.1	–10.4	–10.3
Sales	+17.3	+12.8	+30.1	+25.3
Balance	+15.0	+ 4.7	+19.7	+15.0
1982				
Purchases	–	– 9.4	– 9.4	– 2.5
Sales	+ 3.0	+12.8	+15.8	+ 6.1
Balance	+ 3.0	+ 3.4	+ 6.4	+ 3.7
1983				
Purchases	–16.7	–19.1	–35.8	–20.4
Sales	+ 8.3	+12.9	+21.2	+12.6
Balance	– 8.4	– 6.2	–14.5	– 7.8
1984				
Purchases	–	–30.2	–30.2	– 0.8
Sales	+ 4.7	+ 7.6	+12.3	+ 4.4
Balance	+ 4.7	–22.7	–17.9	+ 3.6
1985				
Purchases	–	–29.6	–29.6	– 0.2
Sales	+ 0.4	+30.8	+31.1	–
Balance	+ 0.4	+ 1.2	+ 1.5	– 0.2
1986				
Purchases	–19.0	–33.6	–52.6	–12.1
Sales	+ 4.1	+76.0	+80.1	+ 3.8
Balance	–14.8	+42.4	+27.6	– 8.4
1987				
Purchases	–	–48.1	–48.1	– 7.3
Sales	+15.0	+62.7	+77.7	+25.4
Balance	+15.0	+14.6	+29.7	+18.1
1988				
Purchases	–	–28.2	–28.2	– 6.1
Sales	–	+16.8	+16.8	–
Balance	–	–11.4	–11.4	– 6.1

*Deutschmark interventions of other central banks participating in the EMS and EMS interventions of the Bundesbank O.S.C. 49;
†From the start of the EMS on 13 March 1979,
+ DM sales (expansionary effect on German liquidity)
– DM purchases (contractionary effect on German liquidity)
Source: Deutsche Bundesbank, *Annual Report* 1986, 1988.

accordance with stability considerations. In this context the Bundesbank has frequently bemoaned the exchange rate passivity of the finance ministers.

Thus, while the EMS may have helped some countries to promote greater monetary discipline domestically, it has made the pursuit of price-stabilizing monetary policy more difficult in Germany.

The road to monetary integration in the EC

In the Single European Act, which became effective in July 1987, the European Community decided on the completion of the internal market by the end of 1992. All internal barriers to the free movement of goods, people, services and capital are to be removed. This new impetus for advancing the economic integration of Western Europe also gave rise to a concert of voices demanding similar progress towards monetary integration. This sentiment was captured at the EC summit in Hanover in June 1988, when the heads of government of the European Community asked a committee under the chairmanship of the president of the EC Commission, Delors, to analyse the prerequisites and consequences of monetary union and to suggest concrete steps for its realization. The 'Delors Report' was completed in April 1989 and served as the basis of discussions at the EC summit in Madrid in June 1989.

This section will set out the German position on monetary integration in the EC as well as some reactions to the Delors Report.

Introduction

In the 1970 discussions on monetary integration, the German authorities belonged to the group of 'economists' rather than to the 'monetarists'. Whereas the 'monetarists' saw monetary integration as the motor of economic and political integration ('L'Europe se fera par la monnaie, ou ne se fera pas'), the 'economists' held that monetary integration can only be introduced when the conditions for a uniform currency are given by a full harmonization of economic and fiscal policies. Although these fronts have softened with time, the two basic philosophies may still be found in the Latin countries on the one hand and the Anglo-German group on the other. The Latin countries have promoted the ECU as a parallel currency and have been keenest on formal steps to limit realignments and on instituting a European central bank which would end the Bundesbank's dominance and reduce the 'deflationary bias of its restrictive policy'. Germany has pleaded for a gradual approach, permitting greater convergence in all policy areas and especially in the commitment to price stability. Currency union, a single currency, a European central bank are seen as a desirable but distant goal. In this context the 'Genscher initiative' of 1988, calling for the timely establishment of a European central bank, must be viewed as the foreign minister's attempt to use the symbol of a common currency to revive the vision of European unification.

The position of the Bundesbank

The Bundesbank has generally remained reserved *vis-à-vis* the host of initiatives for establishing a monetary union in Europe.[4] Recently some of its reserve has been crumbling, however. This applies especially to the Bundesbank's President Pöhl who has become more conciliatory. Other members of the Central Bank Council also seem to have become more sympathetic to EC ideas. Another group within the Council, however, does remain suspicious of proposals to extend or 'improve' the EMS, and of French initiatives in particular. Most such efforts are seen to aim at weakening market mechanisms, undermining the independence of the Bundesbank and reducing the adjustment pressure on countries with weaker currencies. Examples are the demands for greater symmetry, for including Community currencies in German foreign exchange reserves, for joint determination of monetary policy, the extension of credit facilities (Nyborg), and the establishment of the Franco-German Financial and Economic Council (Caesar, 1988, pp. 124–9).

H. Schlesinger, Vice-President of the Bundesbank, has warned of any hasty steps and rash experiments in the very sensitive area of monetary integration in the European Community. Pointing to the twin goals of economic and monetary union specified in the EC Treaty, Schlesinger emphasizes the idea of parallel movement rather than using monetary policy as an instrument of economic union. In this sense closer economic integration is viewed as a prerequisite to the ultimate goal of currency union (Schlesinger, 1989, pp. 2–5).

A monetary or currency union implies that exchange rates are irrevocably fixed and that there are irreversible guarantees for the conversion of any currency into other member currencies and for its transfer into any other country inside and outside the EC. The ultimate fixing of exchange rates must be considered anything but a 'technical measure'. Although such a step is the logical concomitant of monetary integration, it carries wide-reaching political implications. It destroys national autonomy of monetary policy and constrains the decision-making in fiscal and other economic policy areas. The consequences of absolutely fixed exchange rates would be a more or less uniform level of interest rates and common fluctuations of national EC currencies against third currencies. In the end monetary policy for the entire European currency area would have to be determined at the Community level.

Not only in the eyes of the Bundesbank are the prerequisites for such a step still lacking. Considerable differences continue to exist among the individual EC countries – especially regarding a permanently low rate of inflation and the size of the budget deficit. These stand in the way of uniform interest and exchange rates. Unless the causes of the divergencies are removed, a uniform interest and exchange rate policy will necessarily lead to a softening of the high stability standard of Germany.

Fixing the exchange rates also removes an important market mechanism for relieving real economic tensions among the various European regions. Discrepancies in the locational and production conditions must, at fixed exchange rates, be compensated primarily by a flexible and differentiated wage policy. While high mobility of the factors of production can alleviate regional adjustment problems, huge movements of labour from the periphery to the centre cannot be in anybody's interest. If market forces fail, pressures will mount to increase official resource transfers via EC mechanisms. In the long run, convergence of the standards of living within Europe cannot be achieved by public transfers, but by economic development. At the Bundesbank (as at the Netherlands Central Bank and the Bank for International Settlements) the prevailing sentiment is, therefore, that it will take a long time before a uniform monetary and economic policy can be realized.

Given that at the end of the road there will be irrevocably fixed exchange rates, a common currency, and a European central bank, the road to be travelled must be marked. The Bundesbank sets the following important markers:

— Efforts must first be concentrated on the European

financial market which is part of the programme to complete the single market by 1992. This implies free movement of capital and the right of establishment for financial institutions. The major element in a common financial market is the full liberalization of capital movements which – in principle – is to be achieved by mid-1990. This liberalization is to apply 'erga omnes', i.e. against non-EC currencies as well. If everyone is free to decide in which currency he wants to hold his savings, a form of currency competition will ensue in the direction of greater stability. National authorities will no longer be able to lower real interest rates by monetary expansion in order to relieve the burden of government debt or to compensate for excessively high wages and social costs. The major contribution to integration of a liberalization of capital flows, therefore, is that additional mechanisms will become effective – without institutional change – towards a convergence of national policies.

— Initial steps also include the participation of all EC countries in the exchange rate mechanism (at equal conditions) and the endowment of those central banks still lacking sufficient autonomy with greater independence from their governments in preparation for an independent European central banking system.

— Also needed is a further convergence of the 'philosophies' of economic policy and the concepts of market order in the EC countries, which may only be achieved over a longer period of time. While there need not be complete uniformity in countries' economic orders, there must be greater convergence in the ranking of economic policy goals.

— Another prerequisite for progress towards monetary integration is a reduction in the still sharp economic differences among individual EC countries. Mentioned here are the considerable balance of payments imbalances as well as the very different government budget positions, ranging from surpluses in the United Kingdom and Denmark, over countries like Germany and the Netherlands with deficits of 2 to 5 per cent of GNP, to countries like Italy, where deficits exceed 10 per cent of GNP. An important step towards fiscal convergence would consist in waiving the central bank's duty to finance budget deficits.

The position of the Council of Experts to the Federal Ministry for Economic Affairs

The Council (university professors all), in a paper on 'The European monetary order' published in February 1989, puts forward the German position in a thorough analysis of the major points of contention. In this formal presentation the Council sets out the conditions for a European central bank and the road to this ultimate goal.

The following are the minimum requirements for a European central bank which reflect a broad consensus in Germany:

- The European central bank will be obliged to safeguard the purchasing power of the European currency. This obligation will not be weakened in view of other economic policy goals.

- In fulfilling its monetary policy tasks the European central bank should be independent of directives or instructions of the governments as well as other political bodies. This independence is to be guaranteed institutionally by the legal position of the leading personalities of the European central bank.

- The European central bank must not grant loans directly or indirectly to the European Community or its member countries beyond precisely defined narrow limits.

- Safeguarding the independence of the central bank and its obligation to maintain price stability is a difficult task which – unlike most tasks of other policy areas – does not lend itself to federative compromise. Because the European central bank must be truly autonomous, those persons responsible for the European currency must clearly be detached from any particular country's interests.

The Council shares the Bundesbank's opinion that the time is not ripe for a European currency union. In the member countries of the European Community considerable reservations exist towards a surrender of national sovereignty in monetary affairs. And for good reason: past experiences, values, and past practices diverge widely. Hence there is insufficient willingness and ability to have economic policy convergence with price stability. For Germany failure of a premature currency union would mean the loss of coordinated expectations and attitudes geared to a satisfactory measure of price stability – perhaps the most valuable basis of stability policy. Currency union, therefore, remains a distant goal.

Among the three possible strategies of achieving monetary integration (a parallel currency, binding agreements on monetary policy, or a strengthening of the EMS), the Council comes out in favour of the third route.

The Council recommends a strengthening, not a softening, of the necessarily asymmetrical need for greater policy convergence. The prescribed rate of monetary expansion which will some day be determined by the European central bank will in the mean time come from one or more stability-conscious national central banks. It must be made effective for all by an – asymmetrical – adjustment requirement, which is enforced by the limited intervention potential of the still less stability-conscious central banks. To demand more symmetry of adjustment means demanding a softening of the EMS. Such a softening would, however, lead away from the currency union which is to be a union of stability. The problem of asymmetry, the problem of DM dominance, must ultimately be solved by a gradual strengthening of more and more currencies.

Of great importance to a strengthening of the EMS will be the liberalization of capital movements. It will be important, however, to make as little use as possible of the numerous safety clauses and to abolish them in the near future.

The Council emphasizes that the strengthening of the EMS through the agreed removal of all remaining capital controls must not be counteracted by new rules. Such new rules are demanded by several countries under the banner of diminishing the asymmetry of adjustment. They include expanded credit facilities, interventions in Community currencies, Community financing of intramarginal interventions, Community monitoring on the basis of binding indicators, and even the build-up of Community reserves by putting (part of) foreign exchange reserves into a European monetary fund.

Reflecting the 'economist' position, the Council holds that with the growing integration of the EC markets for goods, labour and capital the participating countries' interest in a convergence of monetary policy will increase, even without formal decisions. And with rising investment in the credibility of stability policy the interest in preserving this valuable investment will grow. Soon the same will apply to the national interest in fiscal and wage policies which do not conflict with converging monetary policy.

To the idea of strengthening the EMS corresponds the concept of less and less frequent exchange rate changes. This does not conflict with the Bundesbank's preference for preserving some exchange rate flexibility. Rather, the Council also sees this as a gradual process. As uniform, stability-conscious monetary policy becomes increasingly more reliable, mutual help in defending individual currencies will no longer be considered a policy which will undermine the system, but the legitimate concern with overshooting reactions in disoriented exchange markets.

The Council disagrees with the widely held view that currency union requires harmonization and coordination of fiscal policy and parts of wage and social policies. The postulate of a necessary loss of policy autonomy in other areas besides monetary policy is also usually combined with the thesis that massive international transfers will be required. The Council does not support such views, but holds that economic and monetary integration requires only a limited amount of centrally determined uniform rules or formal, binding coordination of government behaviour in the Community countries.

German responses to the Delors Report

The *Report on Economic and Monetary Union in the European Community* (the Delors Report) is generally viewed with satisfaction in Germany. It reflects many aspects of the German position, including the requirement for an independent central bank, primarily responsible for the maintenance of price stability. The Report suggests a stepwise approach to monetary integration, comprising three phases:

— Phase one would emphasize the full liberalization of capital flows, the completion of a single market in financial services, the participation of all member currencies in the exchange rate mechanism (under uniform rules), and the removal of barriers to the private use of the ECU. The responsibilities of the Committee of Central Bank Presidents would be redefined and a European Reserve Fund established.

— Phase two would establish the principal bodies and structures of the economic and monetary union. It is considered a phase of transition, based on the experiences gathered in phase one and preparing for phase three. In the monetary area it foresees the set-up of the European central banking system, but would leave monetary policy decisions with the national authorities. Reducing the margins of permissible exchange rate fluctuations is possible during this phase.

— Phase three would see the transition to irrevocably fixed exchange rates and the transfer of monetary and economic competencies to Community bodies. Finally, the national currencies would be replaced by a common Community currency.

While this description of the three phases concentrates on the monetary aspects, the Report supports a parallel approach to economic and monetary union, and therefore also describes the economic developments foreseen for each phase.

K.O. Pöhl, the Bundesbank President and a member of the Delors Committee, is confident that the process toward a European Monetary Union is irreversible (Pöhl, 1989). He points to the statement that the Deutschmark's role as the stability anchor of the EMS has been beneficial to all member countries, putting to rest the contention that Bundesbank policy has had a deflationary impact on the EC. Regarding the future course of action, Pöhl emphasizes the need to realize those measures already agreed. Further progress ought to be left to the markets, in which he has more confidence than in the efforts of politicians. He warns, in particular, of too early and ill-prepared head of government conferences and council of minister meetings which try to prepare the surrender of national sovereignty; these would only lead to conflict among the members of the EC. Pöhl opposes the establishment of a European Reserve Fund in phase one. He is critical of the description of the transitional phase two, which he considers the weakest part of the Report. He believes that converging monetary and economic policies are more important prerequisites for a European monetary union than common institutions. Pöhl points to the non-binding nature of the Report and highlights its role as a basis for discussion.

More critical voices can be heard from members of the Central Bank Council and the Council to the Economics Ministry, although they have praise for the thought-provoking prerequisites for the ultimate monetary union as set forth in the Delors Report. They criticize in particular the fact that the Report, while embracing the principle that monetary policy must unambiguously give priority to price stability, suppresses this principle whenever the need for macroeconomic policy mixes and policy coordination is discussed. In their view the

Delors Report overemphasizes formal *ex-ante* coordination; where this involves monetary policy, binding forms of coordination ought to wait until more progress is achieved in price stability convergence. They also insist that stability-oriented monetary policy must not be constrained by the Community's exchange rate policy. They find that the Report relies too much on the 'beneficial' functioning of new institutions, commissions and other Community bodies which will analyse and agree on what is useful for all. Finally, criticism is addressed at the Report's repeated allegations of the need for additional structural and regional policies and additional financing for these purposes.

The Delors Report is a compromise, and as such tries to contain something for every faction. It can serve as a basis for discussing and promoting the necessary steps on the road to full monetary integration. Many aspects of phase one have already been agreed. Other aspects like the strengthening of the Committee of Central Bank Presidents will find favour in Germany, others like the establishment of a European Reserve Fund will be opposed there. Progress towards an economic and monetary union received new impetus from the Single Act. Although the completion of the internal EC market by 1992 does not require monetary union and although economic and monetary integration may not proceed at the same pace, they will reinforce each other as long as the political momentum is maintained.

Notes

1. For a detailed description of the instruments and their effects see Deutsche Bundesbank (1989, p. 45ff.).
2. The European Currency Union was founded in 1972 in response to the exchange-rate arrangements of the Smithsonian Agreement of 18 December 1971. This agreement set a maximum range of fluctuation against the US dollar of ± 2.25 per cent. For non-dollar currencies this implied a total band of ± 9 per cent for fluctuations against each other. Since the EC countries considered such a wide band inconsistent with their ultimate goal of monetary integration, they decided on 21 March 1972 to narrow the range of fluctuation among their currencies to half of that permitted under the Smithsonian Agreement. It is this narrow band which was dubbed 'the snake'.
3. Since February 1973, this component has been excluded from the definition of bank liquidity.
4. These initiatives range from the ideas of the French Finance Minister Balladur to those of the 'New Monnet Committee' (Kohnstamm Group), the 'European Regional Conference', founded

by prominent bankers, politicians and industrialists, the 'Association for the Monetary Union of Europe', suggested by Helmut Schmidt and Giscard d'Estaing, and the 'Intrafractional Working Group European Currency' of the European Parliament (Otmar Franz Initiative), and finally the 'Genscher Initiative' of February 1988.

References

Badura Jürgen, and Otmar Issing (eds) (1980) *Geldpolitik*, Stuttgart.

Borchardt, Knut (1976) 'Währung und Wirtschaft', in Deutsche Bundesbank (1976).

Caesar, Rolf (1988) 'Kontrollierbarkeit der Geldversorgung bei festen Wechselkursen: eine Bilanz der Bundesbankpolitik im Europäischen Währungssystem,' in Claus Köhler and Rüdiger Pohl (eds) *Aspekte der Geldpolitik in Offenen Volkswirtschaften*, Berlin.

Caesar, Rolf (1988) 'Bundesbank-Autonomie: Internationale Bedrohungen?', *Wirtschaftsdienst*, III.

Deutsche Bundesbank (ed.) (1976) *Währung und Wirtschaft in Deutschland 1876–75*, Frankfurt.

(1983) *Deutsche Bankengeschichte*, Vol. 3: *Vom Ersten Weltkrieg bis zur Gegenwart*, Frankfurt.

Deutsche Bundesbank (1987) *Auszüge aus Presseartikeln*, O.S.C. 65, 5 November.

Deutsche Bundesbank (1989) *Die Deutsche Bundesbank – Geldpolitische Aufgaben und Instrumente*, Special Series No. 7, 5th ed (February).

Dudler H.-J. (1984) *Geldpolitik und ihre theoretischen Grundlagen*, Frankfurt.

Dürr Ernst (1973) 'Gelungene Durchkreuzung der restriktiven Geldpolitik', in Dieter Duwendag (ed.) *Macht und Ohnmacht der Bundesbank*, Frankfurt.

Ehrlicher Werner and Simmert Diethard B. (eds) (1982) *Geld- und Währungspolitik in der Bundesrepublik Deutschland*, Supplements to *Kredit und Kapital*, 7, Berlin.

Ehrlicher Werner and Simmert Diethard B. (eds) (1988) *Wandlungen des geldpolitischen Instrumentariums der Deutschen Bundesbank*, Supplements to *Kredit und Kapital*, 10, Berlin.

Emminger, Otmar (1970) 'Zur Problematik der internationalen Geld- und Kapitalbewegungen', *Zeitschrift für das gesamte Kreditwesen*, November.

Emminger, Otmar (1976) 'Deutsche Geld- und Währungspolitik im Spannungsfeld zwischen innerem und äusserem Gleichgewicht (1948–1975)', in Deutsche Bundesbank (ed.) (1976).

Gleske, Leonhard (1988) 'Die Geldmarktpolitik der Bundesbank, Erfahrungen und Probleme', Wolfgang Filc, Lothar Hübl and Rüdiger Pohl (eds) *Herausforderungen der Wirtschaftspolitik*, Berlin.

Gutowski, Armin (ed.) (1987) *Geldpolitische Regelbildung: Theoretische Entwicklungen und empirische Befunde*, schriften des Vereins für Socialpolitik, New Series, Volume 161, Berlin.

Gutowski, Armin (ed.) (1988) *Wechselkursstabilisierung und Währungskooperation*, Schriften des Vereins für Socialpolitik, New Series, Volume 172, Berlin.

Hartwig, Karl-Hans (1984) 'Bundesbankautonomie und Inflationsbekämp-

fung: Politische Ökonomie des Notenbankverhaltens', *List Forum* 12 (May).
Köhler, Klaus (ed.) (1973) *Geldpolitik – kontrovers*, Cologne.
OECD (1973) *Monetary Policy in Germany*, Paris.
Pfleiderer, Otto (1976) 'Die Reichsbank in der Zeit der großen Inflation, die Stabilisierung der Mark und die Aufwertung von Kapitalforderungen', in Deutsche Bundesbank (ed.) (1976).
Pöhl, Karl O. (1989) 'Die Europäische Währungsunion', speech delivered at the Ifo Institute for Economic Research, Munich, June.
Scheide, Joachim (1984) *Geldpolitik, Konjunktur und rationale Erwartungen*, Kieler Studien 188, Tübingen.
Schlesinger, Helmut (1988) 'Das Konzept der Deutschen Bundesbank', in Ehrlicher and Simmert (1988).
Schlesinger, Helmut (1989) 'Die Währungspolitik in der Europäischen Gemeinschaft – aus der Sicht der Deutschen Bundesbank', in Deutsche Bundesbank, *Auszüge aus Presseartikeln*, 7 June.
Spahn, Heinz-Peter (1988) *Bundesbank und Wirtschaftskrise*, Regensburg.
Spindler, Joachim V., Willy Becker and O.-Ernst Starke (1957) *Die Deutsche Bundesbank*, Stuttgart.
Toniolo, Gianni (ed.) (1988) *Central Banks' Independence in Historical Perspective*, Berlin.

3 French monetary policy in the light of European monetary and financial integration

Christian de Boissieu and
Marie-Hélène Duprat

The purpose of this chapter is to provide an overview of French monetary policy in the light of European monetary and financial integration. The European Monetary System (EMS) was created ten years ago. With the implementation of the Single European Act and many European directives, monetary and financial integration will accelerate, perhaps up to the institutional stage of a European central bank, as considered in the recent Delors Report (April 1989).

Three points will be discussed:

- the main elements of change and continuity in the French financial system and monetary policy since the end of the 1970s;
- the impact of the EMS on monetary variables and policy;
- the attitude of French monetary authorities towards European monetary and financial integration.

Elements of change and continuity in the financial system and in monetary policy

Financial innovation and deregulation in France: Where do we stand?

Characteristics of the French financial system in the 1960s and 1970s Until the end of the 1970s, the French financial system could be (and was) analysed by reference to the model of the 'overdraft economy'. Many studies (especially at the Bank of France) elaborated on a distinction, presented by Hicks in 1974, between the 'overdraft economy' and the 'auto-economy' (or, more appropriately, between the overdraft sector and the auto-sector). In an overdraft economy, deficit units do not borrow from the markets (which are non-existent or only residual), but instead rely on bank credit. 'Indirect finance' (i.e. financial intermediation) predominates while 'direct finance' plays a marginal role.

In order to understand the structure of the French financial system, the best starting point is to recall the willingness of monetary authorities right after the Second World War to promote capital formation in a period of economic reconstruction. In accordance with this objective, the financial system was conceived with one basic aim: to keep interest rates low in order to sustain investment spending. In the bond market, the Treasury controlled the interest rates, preventing them from rising enough to clear the market. Hence, a situation of permanent excess demand for funds prevailed in the bond market. Moreover, it is very likely that low interest rates discouraged household saving. The ensuing rationing meant that authorities had to establish priority rules: the first borrower to be satisfied was the Treasury, followed by the set of state-owned financial institutions and industrial enterprises, then came the private financial institutions and finally the private non-financial corporations.

Accordingly, the latter were constantly rationed in the bond market, which thus could play only a marginal role in their funding requirements. They were forced to turn to banks in order to raise funds: a large bank loan market – at the time about four times the size of the bond market – thus emerged. But the banking sphere was also tightly regulated. The system was divided into two parts: a privileged circuit (representing more than 40 per cent of overall bank lending) where loans were extended at preferential rates – this essentially concerned credits for exports, housing, agriculture and various specific projects such as energy-saving investments – and the rest of the system, where interest rates were freely determined by banks.

The clearing of the non-privileged circuit involved the money market and, particularly, the Bank of France. Largely as a result of a banking law dating back to 1945 which imposed the principle of banking specialization,[1] the banking network was markedly heterogeneous: institutions that were structurally either lenders or borrowers coexisted in the money market. Among the latter stood out the investment banks, the non-bank financial institutions and most of the medium- to large-size deposit banks. The structural lenders were the group of small deposit banks and some national banks such as the CDC (Caisse des Dépôts et Consignations) or the CNCA (Caisse Nationale du Credit Agricole). The money market was the place where the two groups could exchange funds. As it turned out, the banking system as a whole exhibited financing needs. The existence of structural borrowers which were particularly vulnerable to reserve shortages forced the Bank of France to meet almost automatically banks' refinancing demand in order to avoid bankruptcies. Thus, the Bank of France ended up as a structural lender in the money market.

The central bank provided the ordinary banks with the necessary amount of reserves at its chosen price. The behaviour of the franc in the exchange market was the driving factor for the setting of money-market interest rates. Authorities frequently manipulated the interest rates in order to stabilize the parity of the franc against the other European currencies, notably in the framework of the 'European monetary snake' (the 'snake' was an early version of the current European Monetary System).

To sum up, there were three main interest rates in the system: one in the bond market, which was maintained artificially low in order to stimulate investment and growth; one in the money market, which was largely assigned to the exchange rate, which, most of the time, entailed keeping the money market rate relatively high – since the franc was often viewed as a weak currency; and finally, the rate on bank credit. As indicated earlier, a substantial proportion of bank lending was extended at below-market rates, but outside this privileged circuit, the rate on bank credit was unregulated.

Indirect finance procedures were dominant until the end of the 1970s. Capital markets were underdeveloped, compared to the United States, the UK or Canada. The money market was the opposite of an 'open market' and the role of the Paris Stock Exchange was marginal in the saving-investment adjustment process. As late as in 1981 financial intermediation represented, on a flow-of-funds basis, close to 80 per cent of total financing in the French economy.

Disintermediation and securitization in France Since the end of the 1970s a dramatic change in the financing structure of the French economy has occurred. Figure 3.1 presents the rate of intermediation in terms of flows, showing a dramatic drop until 1986. The flows are very sensitive to short-run movements (e.g. the drop in disintermediation during 1987, before and after the financial crash (see Figure 3.1).

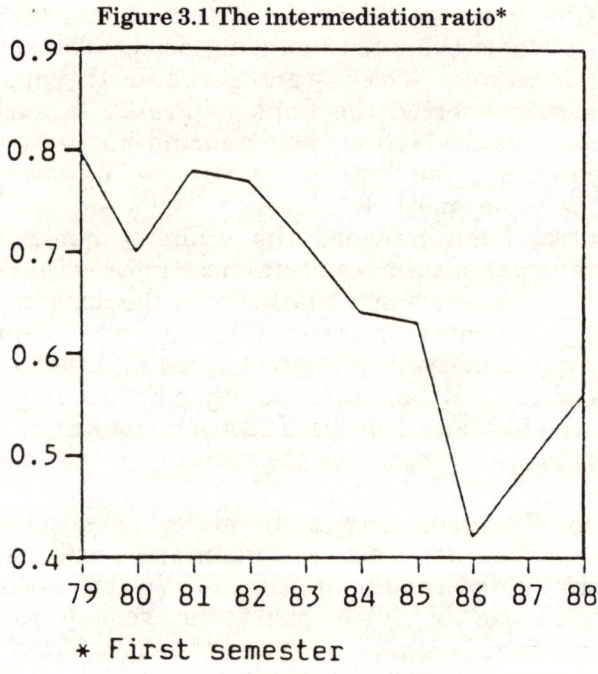

Figure 3.1 The intermediation ratio*

∗ First semester

Source : Bank of France

* This ratio is defined by $\left(\frac{A}{A+B}\right)$, where A is the annual flow of total financing given by credit institutions and B represents total disintermediated financing (commercial paper, Treasury bills, bonds and shares, Euro-credits and Euro-bonds, etc.)

Turning to the structure of corporate financing, we see a parallel development of 'direct finance'. It appears, from a flow-of-funds perspective, that 'direct financing' (i.e. financing through domestic or international capital markets) jumped to 80 per cent in 1986 from 36 per cent in 1981. For 1987, we see the same slowdown – 'direct financing' is close to 64 per cent – which began well ahead of the October crash.

A global securitization ratio which considers from a flow approach the proportion of securities in total financing, has been calculated at the Bank of France. The ratio, which was stable at around 15 per cent during the sub-period 1970–9, jumped to 60 per cent in 1986 and then dropped significantly in 1987 to only 42 per cent.

Securitization began later in France than in the United States or the United Kingdom, but it has developed very rapidly under the influence of a 'catch-up' effect. This phenomenon is illustrated by the portion of commissions and fees in aggregate bank net income, which grew from 15 per cent in 1984 to 25 per cent in 1987.

Another proxy variable for disintermediation and securitization is given by the growth of off-balance sheet operations (back-up lines, standby commitments and letters of credit, swaps, etc.). In December 1987 off-balance sheet operations corresponded to 26.2 per cent of total balance sheet operations, compared with 22.8 per cent at the end of 1980 (for banks reporting to the French Bankers Association). Given the relative inertia of stocks, these figures illustrate the rapid change in the French financial system.

Securitization will accelerate with the gradual implementation of the December 1988 Law creating specialized *fonds communs de créances*. Through such institutional changes, French monetary authorities want to extend competitive pressure in the banking sector and to induce downward adjustments in the intermediation cost. Nevertheless, due to macroeconomic constraints, the authorities have decided to exclude short-term consumer credits from the securitization process which will primarily concern medium and long-term housing credits.

Diversification in the 'menu' of financial instruments was limited in the 1960s and 1970s, compared with the United States or the United Kingdom. Among the few financial innovations during this period were the development of open-ended unit trusts (SICAV: *Sociétés d'investissements à capital variable*) which began in 1963, and a successful diversification of savings instruments with financial intermediaries (particularly contractual savings for housing financing, under the names of *plans d'épargne-logement* and *comptes d'épargne-logement*, which are still very attractive to French households).

In France, most of the new financial instruments have been created in the form and at the time chosen by the monetary authorities (i.e. the Bank of France, the Treasury Department). They correspond to what Christian de Boissieu has called 'public financial innovations', which result from the initiative of the public decision-makers of either directly introducing the new financial instruments or placing restrictions on other parties. Even if the new instruments were satisfying a demand, explicit or latent, by private operators, they resulted from a centralized process. This has been very clear since the start: in 1978, the Monory Act (named after the Minister of Finance) promoted, through tax deductions, the development of the stock market, and this confirms that, in France as in many other countries, financial innovation has sometimes been a tax innovation. A rather paradoxical outcome of the public innovation process was the creation by public decision-makers of the commercial paper market in December 1985. Generally speaking, a commercial paper market gives private agents (lenders and borrowers) some autonomy *vis-à-vis* the banking system and the central bank, and it may reduce the effectiveness of monetary policy by inducing large swings in the velocity of money. Thus it could be seen as paradoxical that monetary authorities took the initiative in this case, but the December 1985 move was also a way of transforming the shadow market for liquidity that had developed since the end of the 1960s ('back-to-back' operations between firms, initiated by them to circumvent credit rationing).

The French experience also confirms that the distinction between private (i.e. decentralized) and public financial innovation is only applicable up to a certain limit. Over a certain threshold of development, a new financial instrument introduced by the monetary authorities is totally subject to market forces (in France, the market for certificates of deposit (CDs) gives an interesting example of this contention; the market has registered a very strong growth: the CDs outstanding totalled 380 billion frs in March 1989, against 65 billion in January 1987).

The acceleration of the financial innovation process in France after 1978 can be explained not only by factors common to all OECD countries (new technologies, the acceleration in the rate of inflation, the subsequent increase in nominal interest rates, and so on) but also by more specific factors:

1. The external constraint on the French banking and financial system: at the end of the 1970s France had to catch up with the leading countries in the field of financial innovation (the United States, the United Kingdom, Canada, etc.), in order to maintain the competitiveness of the French banking system and the role of Paris as a financial centre.

2. The government fiscal constraint: an important aspect concerns coordination of monetary policy and fiscal policy. The constraint associated with monetary targeting by the central bank has led the French Treasury Department to issue new instruments (*obligations renouvelables du Trésor* (ORT), *obligations assimilables du Trésor* (OAT), etc.) in order to finance public-sector deficits through non-monetary means.

3. Financing constraints bearing on certain categories of firms: nationalized firms, small and medium-size enterprises. The 'Delors Act' of January 1983 created several financial instruments (*titres participatifs, certificats d'investissement*, etc.) tailored to nationalized enterprises and small and medium-size enterprises, since they serve to increase the capital of the firm without changing the structure of ownership (these instruments completely separate pecuniary from voting rights).

Table 3.1 gives a chronological list of new financial instruments and markets introduced in France since 1978.

Table 3.1. Main stages of the financial innovation process in France

Date (as from):	
July 1978	Monory Act, which includes tax incentives for the development of the stock market.
July 1989	Creation of mutual funds (*Fonds Communs de Placement*, FCP).
September 1981	Short-term UCITS (Undertakings for Collective Investment in Transferable Securities) (SICAV (Société d'Investissement à Capital Variable) and FCP).
June 1982	LEP (*Livret d'épargne populaire*), a financial instrument offered by all depository institutions to low-income groups, with a ceiling on savings and indexation of the capital on the inflation rate.

January 1983	Delors Act, which creates new financial instruments for the capitalization of nationalized or private firms (and financial institutions): *titres participatifs, certificats d'investissement* etc.
February 1983	Unlisted securities market (*second marché boursier*).
October 1983	CODEVI (*compte pour le developpement industriel*), a financial instrument open to all depository institutions and to all agents. The resources collected through the CODEVIs are channelled to the financing of industry.
March 1985	Negotiable certificates of deposit, denominated in French francs or in foreign currencies (mainly in dollars, sterling, ECUs, etc.).
December 1985	Commercial paper market (*billet de trésorerie*).
January 1986	Negotiable treasury bills (*bons du Trésor négociables* (BTN) and notes issued by specialized financial institutions (*bons des institutions financières spécialisées*).
February 1986	Financial futures market (*Marché à Terme d'Instrument Financier* (MATIF)). Began with a long-term contract (a 'notional' bond with 10-year maturity), supplemented in June 1986 by a short-term contract.
September 1987	Options Market with three underlying securities (Lafarge Coppee, Paribas, Peugeot) at the beginning (*Marché des Options Négociables de Paris* (MONEP)). At present (September 1988), there are eleven underlying securities.
January 1988	The PER (*Plan d'épargne retraite*) corresponding to an individual retirement account, created by an Act of June 1987, is offered, as from this date, to households by credit institutions, insurance companies, pension funds, etc. The PER is equipped with several tax incentives.
September 1988	Future contract on a stock index (with 40 underlying securities), introduced on the MATIF (an option contract on the same index has been offered since the end of 1988).

Financial regulation and deregulation in France

The new Banking Act (1984) From the end of the Second World War until the early 1980s, banking activity in France was governed by a set of regulations adopted in 1941 and largely confirmed in 1945. These regulations, contrary to the German 'universal banking' system, favoured a high degree of specialization and compartmentalization in the French financial system. Due to the increased opening of the French economy, the development of 'direct finance', and a progressive tendency towards universal banking, it was clear in the early 1980s that the 1941–5 legislation had to be updated.

The 1984 Banking Act introduces more uniformity in the French banking sector, by referring to the notion of 'credit institution' (*établissement de crédit*) already introduced in the European Directive adopted in December 1977. Under French law, a credit institution is defined as an institution that engages in at least one of the following three banking operations:

1. collecting deposits from the public;
2. granting credits;
3. issuing means of payment (e.g. credit card, travellers' cheques, banker's drafts).

Without exception, all credit institutions are subject to the same rules (e.g. the same liquidity ratio, solvency ratio, etc.). The broad definition of credit institutions implies that there is no incentive for the development of 'non-bank' banks in France.

Besides the Bank of France and the Ministry of Finance, three bodies are involved in the making of monetary policy or banking regulation:

- The Conseil National du Crédit (National Council of Credit). Under the 1945 law, the CNC had a deliberative power concerning monetary policy and regulations. With the 1984 Banking Act, it has only kept a consultative role on policy issues.
- The Comité de la réglementation bancaire (Committee for Banking Regulation), a deliberative body in charge of banking and financial regulation.
- The Comité des établissements de crédit (Committee of Credit Institutions), which has power to make individual decisions (licensing, etc.).

Some important agents are excluded from the coverage of the Banking Act: the Treasury, the Bank of France, the Caisse des Dépôts et Consignations (which centralizes the deposits with the Caisses d'Epargne and invests them in the financing of social housing, municipalities, and so on) and the postal financial services.

Credit institutions are allowed to engage in activities collateral to their main functions, but various ceilings are imposed to limit the extent of diversification. For example, under a rule adopted by the Committee for Banking Regulation in November 1986, the net income derived from accessory activities (for example insurance business) may not be greater than 10 per cent of the global net product of a credit institution.

The deregulation of interest rates, commissions and fees The first shock of deregulation, which came in 1966–7 with the reform implemented by Michel Debré, then Minister of Finance, consisted of several important steps: the complete liberalization of banks' lending rates, the only remaining constraint being the legal definition of a ceiling for these rates (the ceiling is the usury rate), while deposit rates were kept under a tight control by monetary authorities; and the liberalization of branch banking, which created an intense competition for market shares.

Since May 1986, interest rates on time deposits with a maturity of over three months have been freely determined, and they follow money market rates closely.

Interest payments on demand deposits have been prohibited since 1967. In the present discussion between the banks and their customers, the zero interest rate on demand deposits is seen as the counterpart of free access to many bank services (cheque books, no penalty for small denomination cheques, and so on). In France as elsewhere, this regulation has been circumvented by financial innovation. The UCITS (Under-takings for collective investment in transferable securities), the MATIF (Marché à Terme International de France, the French futures market) and all kinds of cash management techniques generate market interest rates on financial instruments that are close substitutes for demand deposits.

The deregulation of commissions and fees has been, in Paris as in London, an important aspect of the 'big bang'. Besides that, a major change has resulted from the adoption of the Act of January 1988, which adapts the status and the functions of stockbrokers to the new environment.

The removal of exchange controls As far as exchange controls are concerned, the wholesale market has been completely deregulated; there are no longer exchange restrictions on firms and financial institutions. The retail market, however, remains to be deregulated through a phasing out of the last restrictive measures: residents are banned from opening an account abroad and from lending in French francs to non-residents (this regulation has been removed for financial institutions and firms). Some experts consider that the French financial system has already been liberalized, since people may buy foreign securities abroad without any restriction. We disagree with this view. The complete removal of capital controls will create new opportunities for international portfolio diversification and capital movements. The entire deregulation of the retail market may induce a 'qualitative jump'.

Policy innovations: from a direct to an indirect monetary policy

The system innovations described earlier have been logically complemented by policy innovations, i.e. changes in the *modus operandi* of monetary policy. Since the end of the 1950s, France has extensively resorted to a direct control of the money stock through credit ceilings. The ceilings have now been removed and since the end of 1986 the Bank of France has been implementing an indirect monetary policy through interest rate variations.

'Money divisor' and credit control Until the late 1970s, commercial banks had unlimited access to refinancing at the Bank of France. This meant in effect that the supply of credit to the private sector was perfectly elastic at the price fixed by banks. Commercial banks extended loans first, and then turned to the Bank of France to get the central bank money needed to meet the reserve requirement ratio. This meant, in turn, that demand for credit was a powerful determinant of the amount of outstanding credit, and hence of money creation.

Thus, in so far as economic agents fixed the amount of bank credit and ordinary banks, in turn, set the quantity of refinancing with the central bank, the reserve base was ultimately determined by the behaviour of the private non-financial sector. By meeting banks' refinancing demand almost automatically, the Bank of France ended up with little power over the determination of the quantity of central bank balances in the economy. As a consequence, the reserve base could not be relied upon as an instrument of monetary policy and the so-called 'money multiplier' had less relevance in France than what was known as the 'money divisor' – that is the inverse of the traditional money multiplier: commercial banks' share in the issue of monetary liabilities did not result from the refinancing policy of the central bank, but rather from commercial banks' efforts to maximize profits under the constraint of the compulsory reserve ratio. In other words, in France the causality relationship ran from the amount of credit extended by commercial banks to the reserve base rather than the reverse, which is the usual case in most developed countries.

Unable to use the reserve base to carry out its monetary policy, the central bank might have been willing to resort to its intervention rate in the money market. But the manipulation of the money-market rate encountered many difficulties. Firstly, as indicated earlier, the money-market rate was targeted on management of the exchange rate and was thus unavailable for internal regulation purposes. Secondly, relying upon the interest rate to implement monetary policy could have entailed large fluctuations of the rate which could have threatened the stability of the banking system, given its heterogeneity. A strong volatility of the money-market rate would have induced heavy income transfers between structural lenders and borrowers. Thirdly, monetary authorities were concerned to protect the profitability of non-financial firms which were structurally indebted to the banking system.

Hence the Bank of France was left with no other means for implementing monetary control than the resort to some quantitative tools. The foremost quantitative instrument was the so-called *encadrement du crédit* which applied to each bank and combined ceilings on credit growth and penalties – consisting of legal reserve requirements – whenever the limit on credit growth was violated. Once conceived as an apparatus to be used intermittently and for limited periods of time – over the 1958–72 period, a discontinuous quantitative policy took place, with ceilings being phased in (1958–9, 1963–5 and 1968–70) and out – the *encadrement* was actually continuously exercised from 1972 to 1985, even if it was sometimes somewhat relaxed (for example the expansionary programme of Jacques Chirac in the fall of 1975).

Lessons from the experience with credit ceilings Some lessons may be drawn from the French experience:

(a) A basic idea behind the whole device was to enable the Bank of France to separate out the control of the money supply from the interest rate policy and to pursue three different objectives at the same time: defending the exchange rate with the money-market rate; promoting investment via controlled interest rates; keeping money growth within specified targets through the *encadrement du crédit*.

(b) The growth of the money stock has been rapid despite the ceilings. Between 1972 and 1976, the average growth of M2 was well above the growth of nominal GDP and around 16 per cent.

(c) During the period under review, ceilings were not always binding. The Bank of France has calculated an indicator of credit rationing as a combination of objective and subjective information. It shows the sub-periods when the quantitative constraint on credit has been effective.

(d) When there was some credit rationing, non-financial agents (firms and households) were induced to circumvent it through domestic channels (such as trade credit, commercial paper procedures), which tended to accelerate the velocity of money. For the 1970s the correlation between the transaction velocity of M1 (calculated by the Bank of France) and the indicator of credit rationing was close to one when credit ceilings were binding. The tightness of exchange restrictions limited the external loopholes to credit ceilings (for example borrowing on international capital markets, leads and lags).

(e) Theoretically, credit ceilings could be interpreted as a substitute for an interest rate increase (credit rationing replaced price rationing). International comparisons for the 1970s show that France did not significantly 'economize' on the level of interest rates with the credit ceilings. They reduced the fluctuation more than the level of domestic interest rates.

(f) The selectivity of credit ceilings (export credits, some agricultural and housing credits were not subject to them) was another loophole which reduced the effectiveness of direct monetary policy.

(g) Credit ceilings 'froze' banks' market shares and banking competition, but perhaps less than is usually claimed. During the period 1973–84, banking competition continued through financial instruments which were not directly exposed to quantitative constraints (such as exonerated credits).

The shift to an indirect monetary policy France, like some other developed countries, removed credit ceilings in the mid-1980s. The gradual phasing out of exchange restrictions was a good argument for lifting the quantitative constraint on credit: in an open economy with increasing international capital mobility, the effectiveness of credit ceilings is nil or negligible, since firms and other economic agents can borrow on international markets.

As early as 1984 the government announced the dismantling of the *encadrement du crédit*. In a first stage however, the new device – enforced in January 1985 – mostly consisted in quantitative control: banks were under the obligation to form reserves on their assets at a very progressive rate. This apparatus was intended to be a safeguard during the transition years towards the implementation of money-market operating procedures, which took place in January 1987. By 1985, the money market was still too compartmentalized for the central bank to be able to conduct market-based techniques to exercise monetary control.

The existence of a fluid, deep money market able to respond swiftly to impulses from the central bank is a prerequisite for the effectiveness of a market mode of monetary regulation. But until the mid-1980s the French money market was heavily regulated and significantly restricted in terms of participants and of types of securities. Hence, for the Bank of France to be able to conduct a market-based monetary policy efficiently, extensive financial reorganization was needed.

The reform of the money market occurred in December 1986. An important measure to be enforced was the abolition of the morning day-to-day money-market rate fixing, which means that the day-to-day money rate is liable to fluctuate more within the day than it did in the past. In addition, the former interbank market has been split into two sections, one reserved for banks and one accessible to all economic agents. Within the new interbank market, authorities have gradually dismantled the former access of banks to the Bank of France with privileged forms of paper. Otherwise, banks could have escaped the impact of open-market operations. However, the most important changes concerned the other section of the money market. While it used to be very restricted both in terms of participants (for example, firms could neither lend nor borrow directly in the market) and in terms of securities, it is today open to all economic agents. Further, it now allows participants to trade a broad set of assets with maturities ranging from ten days to seven years. Moreover, in February 1986, an interest futures market was created and shortly after this a currency futures market was set up.

To implement its monetary policy, the central bank continues to intervene mainly in the interbank market. The main technique consists in changing the key rate of intervention. This operating procedure is supplemented by the use of reserve requirements and by occasional open-market operations – which consist in controlling the supply of reserves to the banking system and leaving the interest rate to adjust freely.

The Bank of France seeks to exercise a tight control over very short-term interest rates, hoping that these will drive other interest rates in the desired direction. An active interest rate policy benefits today from more favourable conditions than those of the 1970s. On the one hand, the financing requirements of domestic firms have been steadily decreasing and their financial situation has markedly improved, which allows them to bear higher levels of or larger fluctuations in interest rates than in the past. On the other hand, the heterogeneity of the banking system, regarded for many years as a major obstacle to an active interest rate policy, is progressively decreasing as banks now tend to be more or less on an equal footing for collecting resources or providing loans. Further, the expansion and the diversification of capital markets make the matching of their claims and liabilities possible (matched maturities and so on) and should permit a decline in the intermediation risk (interest rate and illiquidity risk).

The central bank's interventions on the money market take the form of either periodic calls for offer or short-term repurchase agreements ('pension' facilities) at a penalty rate (these transactions were being conducted through seven-day repurchase agreements up until August 1988 when the Bank of France, in a context of uncertainty about the behaviour of money-market rates, proposed five and ten-day maturities to the banks).[3] The former procedure is used by far the most often. The latter allows banks to acquire reserves on their own initiative at a rate which normally stands above money-market rates. Banks usually resort to pension facilities in cases of tension on the call-money market. In principle, these facilities set an upper limit to fluctuations in the day-to-day interest rate. Normally, the day-to-day interbank money-market rate stands between the call for tender rate and the pension rate.

In addition to the manipulation of its key rates, the Bank of France may influence developments in short-term interest rates by engaging in 'pure' open-market operations. Indeed, the central bank tends to provide reserves to the banking system, occasionally playing on the quantity of central bank money and leaving the interbank interest rate to fluctuate according to the law of supply and demand. This type of intervention is conducted by means of very short-term repurchase agreements (24 to 48 hours) or purchases and sales of Treasury bills. The main purpose of these punctual operations is to ensure that the money market functions smoothly. More precisely, they are intended to ensure that loan institutions do not run into difficulty in meeting their reserve requirements or that they can offset unexpected reserve shortages which would be likely to cause large gyrations in money-market interest rates.

The experience of 1987–9 with this new operating rule leads to the following:

(a) In France, as elsewhere, policy concerning reserve requirements has not been very active during the last two years (see Table 3.2). Reserve ratios are relatively stable over time and low by some international standards (5 per cent on demand deposits, 2.5 per cent on time deposits, saving accounts and related financial instruments as of May 1989).

Table 3.2. Changes in the reserve requirement rates

Reserve requirement rates applied (%)	End December 1987	From 1 January 1988
French franc resident deposits		
Demand deposits	5	5
Time deposits		
(*Comptes sur livrets*)	1	2.5
Other claims	2	2.5

Source: Banque de France, *Compte Rendu* (1988).

(b) The open-market policy is not very active in France. To be sure, the money market has been opened to non-financial agents (for example firms) since 1985–6. But the secondary market for Treasury bills is thin, since commercial banks are now inclined to keep the T-bills they buy on the primary market. Since the secondary market is neither deep nor resilient, the Bank of France cannot take the risk of damaging it with huge interventions.

(c) Several constraints put a *de facto* limit to interest rate flexibility. Some limits are domestic: compulsory reserves cannot be changed significantly in an economy where disintermediation grows rapidly, since they create a distortion between direct and indirect financing procedures. Most limits are external.

Continuity in the status of the Central Bank

Institutional considerations The Bank of France has a large role as defined by Article 1 of the January 1973 law, which still applies:

The Bank of France is the institution which, in the framework of the economic and financial policy of the nation, receives from the State the general mission of supervising money and credit. On this ground, it watches over the proper working of the banking system. The Bank of France's capital belongs to the state.[4]

The French central bank has thus a traditional and customary role. The peculiarity of the French system lies in the fact that this role is exercised under the wing of the Ministry of Finance, as is apparent in Article 3:

On behalf of the State and in accordance with the general instructions given by the Minister of Economy and Finance, the Bank of France regulates the relations between the franc and foreign currencies and manages the official foreign exchange reserves. The Bank may participate, with the authorisation of the Minister of Finance, in international monetary agreements.[5]

The independence of the Bank of France is a recurrent theme in the economic and political debate. Compared with the Bundesbank or with the Board of Governors of the Federal Reserve System, the French central bank has no real autonomy with respect to the Ministry of Finance (especially, with respect to the Direction du Trésor). Besides the fact that the governor is appointed by the government and can be dismissed at its discretion, the Minister of Finance appoints the members of the ruling bodies: the General Council (Conseil Général), the National Council of Credit, the Committee for Banking Regulation and the Committee of Credit Institutions. The dependence of the Bank of France does not necessarily mean the submission of monetary policy to fiscal policy. It depends on general circumstances, personal credibility and the personal relationship between the Minister of Finance and the governor of the Bank of France. In the past, the institutional structure may have encouraged the monetization of budget deficits (during some fiscal years in the 1950s or the mid-1970s). But this cannot be taken as a general rule. Since the end of the 1970s, the Ministry of Finance has been keen to accelerate the pace of financial innovation and to promote the development of capital markets, in order to rely on non-monetary financing for public deficits.

The independence of the Bank of France was a political issue just before the general election of 1986. Afterwards, the Chirac government, despite some informal commitments, did not implement any change in the institutional framework. For a long time the appointment of able and credible people at the head of the central bank has been regarded as a good substitute for institutional reform. The French experience suggests that this approach could be misleading, and that the functional perspective cannot in the end be disconnected from the institutional one. General aspects of the contemporary debate about a future European central bank are related to the autonomy of this bank and the monetary–fiscal mix at the European level.

Moral suasion in the implementation of French monetary policy
Moral suasion exists everywhere, but channels may vary from one country to another. In France, moral suasion is exercised on commercial banks by the Direction du Trésor, the Bank of France and the Banking Commission (in charge of the implementation of regulations and prudential control). Some other public institutions, such as the Caisse des Dépôts et Consignations, have a key position and may exert some influence on other financial and non-financial institutions.

In France, moral suasion is reinforced by the fact that many bank managers are former high civil servants, and that they keep a close relationship with the Ministry of Finance. In principle, this has also fluctuated with the state of ownership, namely with the waves of nationalization and privatization.

In 1982, the Socialist government justified the nationalization of banks by its desire to influence the objective function of the banking firms in a direction more favourable to the financing of small and medium enterprises and by the need to articulate more clearly both industrial and monetary policy. The results have been rather disappointing. In 1986, the Conservative government justified privatization (the process of privatization stopped at the end of 1987 with the October financial crash and the change in political majority in June 1988) by the pressures of competition and by the needs for French credit institutions to raise their capital. It is too early to assess the fulfilment of these goals. The question of ownership is relevant when analysing the distribution of resources and profit among activities and among agents. It does not always give accurate information about the distribution of power. This is one lesson to be drawn from the French experience. Before the implementation of the 1982 nationalization programme, the actual control of the banking sector by the monetary authorities was already stringent through 'moral suasion'. The change in ownership resulting from privatization does not necessarily mean less influence for the monetary authorities. Everything depends on the practical use of 'moral suasion'.

The impact of the EMS on monetary variables and on monetary policy

General remarks

Before assessing the evolution of French monetary policy, four elements must be considered:

1. Since the creation of the EMS in 1979, the stability of intra-European parities has been conditioned mostly by the fluctuations of the dollar. The substitutability is higher between the dollar and the Deutschmark than between the dollar and the French franc. Thereby, when the dollar drops, the Deutschmark usually rises against the franc, which drives the Bank of France to raise domestic interest rates in order to keep the parity. This phenomenon does not constitute a general principle, but it has often occurred (for instance, the April 1986 and January 1987 realignments in the exchange rate mechanism of the EMS must be related to the fall of the dollar).

In other circumstances, substitutability between the dollar and the Deutschmark was lower, and intra-European parities were more sheltered from the drop in the dollar. This was illustrated several times during the period 1988–9, due to tax measures introduced in West Germany, to political considerations, and so on.

In other words, the external constraint on French monetary policy has often been conditioned by the level and the change in the US currency, because of recurrent shifts in international portfolios.

2. The implementation of tight capital controls until 1986 allowed a 'decoupling' of money-market rates in Paris and rates on the Euro-franc market during the periods of speculative

attack on the franc. The most impressive example occurred just before the parity realignment of March 1983, with the Euro-rates reaching a peak of 5,000 per cent (annual rate). During this episode, it is likely that the Bank of France asked some nationalized banks to borrow on the Euro-franc market in order to discourage speculation by raising interest rates. Since 1986, the segmentation of the domestic market and the Euro-market has dramatically diminished.

3. The stance of monetary policy is not completely independent of its *modus operandi*. The phasing out of credit ceilings in the middle of the 1980s does not mean the implementation of a more accommodating monetary policy. It indicates the desire to abandon the 'overdetermination' of the financial system by monetary authorities (i.e. a situation where the authorities control the prices and the volumes on the credit market), and to rely more on price effects.

4. French authorities have always exhibited a strong preference for monetary gradualism, based on uncertainty about the transmission mechanism and the fear that 'shock therapy' would have more impact on the employment level than on the inflation rate.

The hierarchy of the ultimate goals

The main phases since the mid-1970s The years 1976–7 represented a turning point for French monetary policy. During the period 1971–5, the growth of the money stock was rapid, especially after the first oil shock, in order to offset the ensuing deflationary impact. In the fall of 1975, the Chirac government implemented a reflationary monetary–fiscal mix, which had a limited effect on real growth and unemployment but boosted inflation. Then, taking office as prime minister in the summer of 1976, Mr Barre announced an economic package relying on a gradual tightening of credit. Over the period 1976–89, five sub-periods may be distinguished:

(a) *1977–9*: implementation of the Barre economic pro-gramme, under a floating franc. The credibility of the monetary–fiscal mix explains the relative stability of the franc during this sub-period.

(b) *1979–81*: the creation of the EMS and the second oil shock, both requiring a more restrictive monetary policy, and the *de facto* alignment of French monetary policy on German policy.

(c) *1981–3*: a 'free-rider' economic policy implemented by the

Socialist government, with the aim of circumventing the external constraint on the French economy and of favouring ultimate goals in real terms (real growth; the level of employment). Owing to the decoupling of French economic policy from that of the rest of the world, this experience ended in March 1983. The failure of the 1981–3 attempt to pursue isolated economic expansion has actually had far-reaching consequences for the conduct of French monetary policy. It showed in a striking way the limits of France's independence as regards its economic policy. Over the 1981–2 period, Germany markedly reduced its inflation rate while France allowed a build-up of inflation. The ensuing increase in the inflation differential between the two countries brought about both repeated realignments (three between October 1981 and March 1983) and significant changes in competitiveness between realignments. To avoid encouraging the drifting of the EMS into a 'crawling peg' regime following the March 1983 realignment and the concomitant balance of payments crisis, France had to choose one of these three options: to withdraw from the EMS, to ask for wider margins of fluctuation or to reduce its rate of inflation in order to thwart the growing inflation discrepancy with Germany. The first option was much debated and finally rejected, the second was never envisaged, so the fight against inflation became France's only possible option. The French authorities then decided that given the growing internationalization of the economy and the ensuing loss of economic policy autonomy, it was preferable to accept the EMS discipline and constraint rather than vainly oppose structural integration trends. Accordingly, France has markedly intensified monetary coordination within the EMS setting. Since then, monetary policy has been geared mainly to defending the franc parity within the EMS, with the intention of turning the franc into a strong currency.

(d) *1983–5*: a return to orthodox economic policy and to the disinflation target, with a rising dollar (until February 1985). Monetary policy then gained much credit as an instrument of the fight against inflation. More specifically, it was thought that by maintaining the agreed-upon parity of the franc with the Deutschmark, France imposed on itself a monetary discipline which would contribute to the defeat of inflation. Further, there is a view according to which France, by linking its monetary policy to that of Germany through the EMS, put itself in a position to 'borrow' the Bundesbank credibility in the area of financial discipline with the anticipated result of breaking the inflationary expectations of the private sector. German monetary policy became *the* anchor for French monetary policy. Since 1983, money growth has declined and inflation has rapidly decreased (from 1984 onwards, inflation has stood at 2.5–3 per cent). But as the marked slowdown of inflation is a feature shared by most European countries over this period, it is tricky to attribute it entirely to the enforcement of the exchange-rate-oriented monetary policy.

(e) *1985–9*: during this last sub-period, disinflation remained the prominent ultimate goal, under new circumstances (the drop in the dollar from early 1985 to early 1988; the gradual phasing out, in France, of credit ceilings). German interest rates remain the reference for French rates, at least for the short-term rates.

The reaction function of the Bank of France Among several empirical analyses of the reaction function of the central bank, the article by P. Artus *et al* (1987) presents interesting and widely accepted conclusions. In this study, the money-market interest rate (the dependent variable) is explained by a reduced-form equation where the explanatory variables are the following:

— the money-market rate in Germany;
— the Euro-dollar rate;
— the ratio of the actual money stock over the target for that money stock (a gap between the two variables is supposed to induce some adjustment in interest rates);
— the ratio of foreign exchange reserves to imports (the central bank increases domestic rates when this ratio drops);
— the gap between the actual exchange rate of the Deutschmark and the French franc and the central EMS parity. The Bank of France is supposed to adjust domestic rates in order to avoid the depreciation of the franc, and interest rate policy is a substitute for intramarginal interventions;
— the change in the exchange rate of the franc *vis-à-vis* the dollar;
— the growth rate of the consumers' price index (CPI);
— a dummy variable representing the effect of the 1981 presidential elections.

Estimated with monthly data for the period 1979–85, the reaction function confirms the characteristics of the phases described in the preceding section. The weight given to German

Table 3.3. Intermediate monetary targets and nominal GDP

	1977	1978	1979	1980	1981	1982	1983	1984	1985	1986*	1987	1988
Official targets	M2	M2	M2	M2	M2	M2	M2	M2	M2	M3	M2 and M3	M2
Announced range	12.5	12.0	11.0	11.0	10.0	12.5– 13.5	10.0	5.5– 6.5	4.0– 6.0	3.0– 5.0	4.0– 6.0(M2) 3.0– 5.0(M3)	4.0– 6.0
Actual growth of target	14.0	12.1	14.4	9.8	11.4	11.5	10.2	7.6	6.9	4.6	4.0(M2) 9.1(M3)	5.0
Growth of nominal GDP	12.3	13.6	14.1	13.4	12.3	14.7	10.3	8.8	7.1	7.3	5.0	6.7

* A new system of monetary aggregates was introduced in 1986.

rates has increased significantly with the creation of the EMS in 1979. The rate of inflation became one of the most powerful variables after the turning point of 1983.

Intermediate targets of French monetary policy

Official targets Table 3.3 provides an overview of the intermediate targets publicly announced by the Bank of France, and compares them with the actual monetary growth and the growth in nominal GDP. This table gives rise to two considerations.

Firstly, a former Governor of the Bank of France, R. de La Genière, has characterized French monetary policy as 'quantitative, pluralist and gradualist'.

We will come back later to pluralism. As far as the 'quantitative' dimension is concerned, the French monetary authorities have been keen, since 1977, to reduce the liquidity ratio (i.e. the ratio of money stock to nominal GDP). Table 3.3 confirms that this ratio has dropped rapidly since 1980 for the aggregate M2. But the goal of monetary authorities has been rather ambiguous, since the liquidity ratio (the inverse of the income/velocity of money) is more under the control of private agents than under the control of the central bank, and since a monetary aggregate such as M2 gives a biased view of the financing of the French economy (since the end of the 1970s, the growth of M2 has slowed down not only because of the stance of monetary policy, but also because of the development of capital markets and associated portfolio shifts: see Table 3.3.

Table 3.3 also illustrates the gradualism of French monetary policy. The greatest discontinuity in monetary targeting occurred at the end of 1983 when the target announced for 1984 was about half of that set for the previous year. This break corresponds to the decision taken by the Socialist government to keep the franc within the exchange rate mechanism (ERM) of the EMS, and to implement a tight incomes policy.

Secondly, did external constraint, in particular the ERM of the EMS, induce a gap between the targets and actual money growth? This question relates to possible conflicts (and trade-offs) between the exchange rate target (which is official in the ERM) and interest rate or money growth targets. The Bank of France usually analyses the growth of the money stock with the 'counterparts' of this stock (i.e. the claims which appear on the asset side of the balance sheet of the aggregate banking sector). The external counterpart of the money stock corresponds to claims on the rest of the world held by the central bank or commercial banks. Under fixed exchange rates, fluctuations in the external counterpart (caused by official intervention on the foreign exchange market) affect the money stock growth, unless the central bank can sterilize capital inflow or outflow. The effectiveness of sterilization policies is heavily dependent on the degree of currency substitution at the international level. To be sure, the phasing out of capital controls will extend currency substitution and therefore reduce in the future, perhaps to zero, the effectiveness of sterilization policies.

Coming back to the French case, the year 1985 is a clear example of monetary overshooting due mainly to external factors. In 1985, the aggregate M2 increased by 6.9 per cent, above the target which had been announced (4–6 per cent). Capital inflows which took place until the middle of 1985 have been sterilized to a very limited extent. The growth in the external counterpart of the money stock was not offset by a slowdown in the expansion of domestic credit.

Conversely, the overshooting in 1987 had nothing to do with capital movements and the ERM. It came from the acceleration of domestic credit (particularly credit to private agents), and also from the 'flight to liquidity' which began in early 1987, well ahead of the October stock market crash.

The counterparts of the money stock (claims on the rest of the world, claims on the Treasury, claims on private agents) are somewhat interdependent. But the French experience confirms that for a country belonging to a currency area with fixed (and adjustable) exchange rates and great capital mobility, sterilization policy could not be very effective.

Unofficial targets In the early 1980s, given the process of financial innovation and the further stages in European integration, the Bank of France decided to be 'pluralist' and to monitor other monetary targets besides the official one. Three sets of variables were taken into consideration:

1. Other monetary aggregates. Financial innovation and the development of direct financing procedures led the central bank to monitor wider monetary aggregates such as M3 or L (the total of liquid assets).[6] Given the regulation on deposit rates and the intense shifts in portfolios, the growth of large monetary aggregates has substantially exceeded the expansion of M2 over the past three years.

2.   Credit aggregates. This kind of aggregate is likely to be more sheltered from financial innovations than monetary aggregates. Since domestic credit expansion (DCE) is a narrow concept, the Bank of France has progressively paid attention to global credit, a larger aggregate that adds to DCE the non-monetary sources of financing. Global credit, treating on the same basis domestic and international financial operations, is well adapted to the new world of financial globalization.

3.   Exchange rates. In addition to the official parities of the ERM, France has been keen to promote and respect target zones at the international level. The target zones are official within the group of seven major industrialized countries (G-7), but not publicly announced outside. The exchange rate of the franc *vis-à-vis* the dollar has to be introduced in the reaction function of the Bank of France (see p. 72). Not only did France play an instrumental role in the signature of the Louvre Accord (February 1987), but it is also advocating further steps in the direction of more stable exchange rates. The issue concerns the coordination exercise, but also the recurrent debate about the adjustment process: in the face of domestic or external shocks, how can the burden of adjustment be shared between economic variables (nominal exchange rates, real exchange rates, interest rates, real growth, employment, and so on) and the related markets?

The instruments: interest rate policy in France

The shift from a direct to an indirect monetary policy (see p. 63) does not mean that the central bank is in position to set domestic rates at the level required by domestic goals. We have seen that the reaction function combines internal and external targets, and may imply at some point a trade-off between these two objectives.

The level of interest rates The correlation between short-term rates in France, the US and Germany has been high in the medium and long term (see Figure 3.2(a)), and reinforced in the recent past (see Figure 3.2(b)).

The increased integration of financial markets has also induced a greater correlation between long-term rates (see Figure 3.3).

Whatever the portion of the yield curve considered, there is a

Figure 3.2 Money-market rates

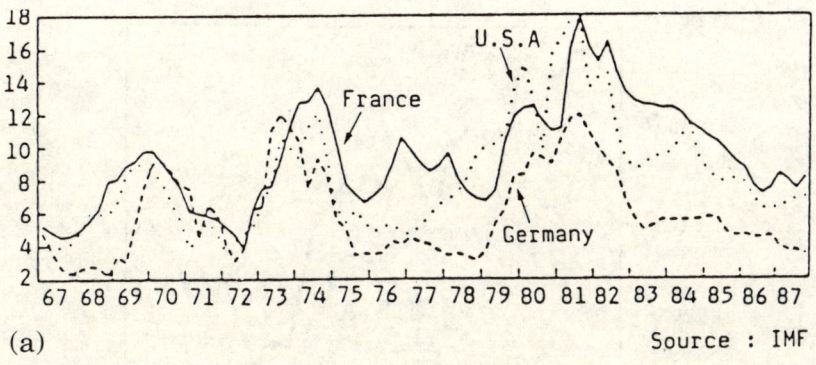

(a)   Source : IMF

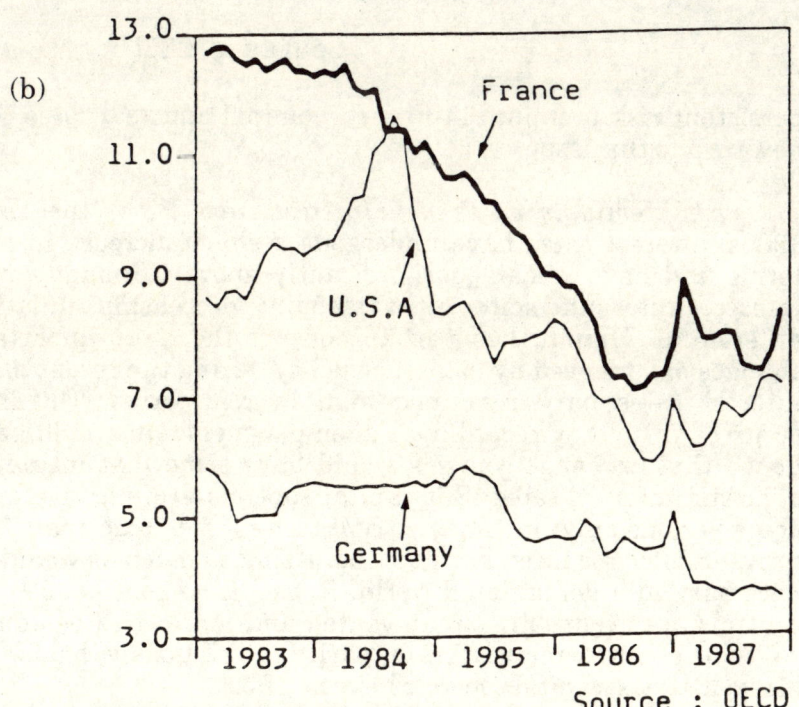

(b)

Source : OECD

Figure 3.3 Bond yields

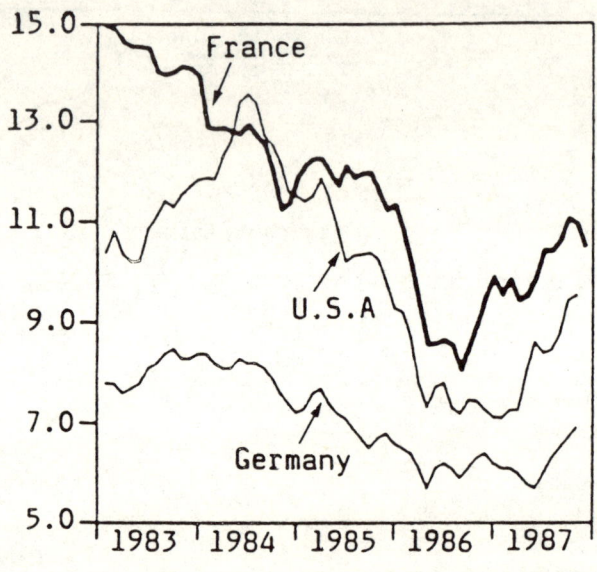

Source : OECD

persistent risk premium in French nominal and real rates. We now turn to this issue.

The risk premiums in French interest rates Since the early 1980s, interest rates have undergone a sharp increase in real terms and have remained significantly above Germany's real interest rates in spite of a steadily decreasing inflation differential. Herein, lies perhaps one of the most important changes experienced by monetary policy during the recent past: interest rates have remained high in real terms. This has occurred in spite of record high unemployment. One could have hoped that exchange controls would have somewhat insulated domestic interest rates. But capital controls are effective over short periods only: in times of EMS crises, it is true that they prevent domestic interest rates from rising as much as would be necessary in a deregulated world. But as time goes by, capital controls are eventually circumvented and interest rates adjust so that covered interest rate parity continuously holds. In 'normal' times, capital controls have no effect.

The real interest rate gap with Germany (which has stood at 150 and 200 basis points) must be interpreted as a credibility gap. International investors still require a risk premium when investing in French francs. There is a wide and persistent discrepancy between the recent performance of the French economy (especially as far as inflation and wage costs are concerned), and the perception by international investors. To reduce and perhaps to remove this risk premium, French economic policy has to be not only reasonable (a condition which is satisfied) but also predictable over time (a more open issue). In 1982, and also more recently, some experts have claimed that the way to suppress the interest rate differential between Germany and France is for the latter to leave the ERM of the EMS. This is pure illusion, since the floating of the franc would accelerate domestic inflation (for a contestable currency, floating means a risk of a cumulative depreciation) and create upward pressure on domestic interest rates.

The required continuity does not only concern the monetary–fiscal mix; it also applies to more structural issues, such as the ownership of firms. In this respect, the cycle of nationalization and privatization in the 1980s may have decreased the global credibility of the country, and may therefore have contributed to the high level of risk premiums in French interest rates.

The coordination between monetary policy and other tools of economic policy

Monetary policy and fiscal policy Table 3.4 presents the OECD data concerning the breakdown of actual budget balances (for the entire public sector, not only for the state) in two components (cyclical and structural). The data illustrates the reflationary fiscal measures during the sub-period 1981–2, which were reinforced by accommodating monetary policies. Since 1983, positive signs of the variations in the structural budget balance have confirmed the desire to increase credibility and to share the burden of adjustment between monetary policy and fiscal policy.

Another aspect of the monetary–fiscal mix concerns the financing of budget deficits. Since the end of the 1970s, French authorities have relied more on markets than on money creation, given the constraints associated with monetary targeting. The monetization of the public debt has been negligible in France since 1983–4. However, the analysis of monetization is rather difficult. With financial innovations and the opening of the money market to non-financial agents (such

Table 3.4. Budget balances: France (as % of GDP)

	1980	1981	1982	1983	1984	1985	1986	1987	1988	1989*
Changes in actual balances	+0.9	−2.0	−0.9	−0.3	+0.2	+0.3	−0.1	+0.8	+0.7	0
Part due to cyclical components	−0.4	−1.0	−0.4	−0.6	−0.3	−0.3	0	−0.1	+0.6	+0.4
Changes in structural balances	+1.3	−1.0	−0.6	+0.2	+0.4	+0.6	0	+0.9	+0.1	−0.4

* forecast

Source: OECD (+ means budgetary and fiscal restrictions and a move towards a surplus; − means budgetary and fiscal expansion and a move towards a deficit).

NB: Because of approximations, the sum of the figures in the last two rows is not always equal to the figures in the first row.

as firms or households), the distinction between monetary and non-monetary financing of public deficits has become somewhat academic.

Monetary policy and incomes policy Up until the mid-1970s, money creation was not viewed as playing a major role in the development of inflation. Inflation was believed to be largely inertial and to result mainly from excessive costs of production: the wage shock of 1968, wage indexation, the existence of a minimum wage which was continuously raised in real terms, the oil shocks, were thought to account for most of inflation. Hence the fight against inflation hardly involved the containment of money creation but relied mainly on incomes policy, in particular price controls. However, concern with the link between money growth and inflation ultimately surfaced and, in 1977, monetary authorities began to set money growth targets. Since then, the growth rate of the money supply has been stabilized.

When it was introduced by the Barre programme at the end of 1976, monetary targeting was intended to be a substitute for a formal incomes policy, which it was quite impossible to implement at this time for political reasons. In affect, contrary to what occurred at the same period in West Germany, the announcement effect of monetary targeting on employers and unions has been negligible. Even today they remain very limited, whilst the announcement effect on international operators and the foreign exchange market seem to be crucial. Nevertheless, the tightening of monetary policy after 1983 was necessary (but not sufficient) for the success of the disindexation policy.

Monetary policy and industrial policy In considering the debate on the nationalization of banks, we alluded to the links between monetary and industrial policy. Another dimension must be considered, which concerns the high degree of selectivity of French monetary policy. The proportion of subsidized credits – which involve agriculture, housing, exports and some invest-ment expenditure – of the total amount of credits was 42 per cent in 1975, 44.6 per cent in 1984, and again 42 per cent at the end of 1987. Behind the apparent stability in the proportion of subsidized credits (which reflects also a stock-flow adjustment problem), the share of those credits *de jure* or *de facto* indexed on market rates has significantly increased. This necessary evolution is a way of reconciling some monetary selectivity on the one hand with market mechanisms and the constraints associated with European integration on the other. No doubt, financial liberalization will inevitably loosen the links between monetary policy and industrial policy which have constituted a structural feature of the French system.

The attitude of French monetary authorities towards European monetary and financial integration

France and the issue of asymmetry within the EMS

When they refer to the argument of asymmetry, analysts have in mind several features of the working of the EMS:

1. The asymmetry in the objective function of national policy-makers;
2. The asymmetry in the adjustment process of hard-currency countries and weak-currency countries;
3. The asymmetry between countries in deficit and countries in surplus, which is often a particular aspect of (2).

Here, we shall insist on dimensions (2) and (3), but also mention the asymmetry in collective preferences.

Hard-currency countries and weak-currency countries The EMS zone is mainly a Deutschmark zone, and this situation confers duties but also privileges on West Germany. Germany, as the most virtuous country (at least, in terms of disinflation and external surplus), sets the tone for the other member countries.

The set of hard currency countries includes, besides West Germany, the Netherlands and countries closely connected with the EC without belonging to it (for example Switzerland and Austria). All these countries peg their currency to the Deutschmark and follow its upward movements (the pegging of the Belgium franc to the Deutschmark is too recent to be mentioned).

The analogy often presented between the role of West Germany in the EMS and the role of the United States under Bretton Woods is valid only to a certain extent. German economic policy, particularly German monetary policy, is the anchor for other member countries' economic policy, as is still the case for US economic policy at the world level. But the country issuing the reserve currency of the zone has not exactly the same kind of responsibilities if it is in a permanent deficit (see the case of the US) or in a permanent surplus (West Germany).

For France, the asymmetry is manifest in several aspects:

1. The frontier between hard-currency countries and weak-currency countries is rather rigid. The former are exposed to the well-known virtuous circle (revaluation–disinflation–revaluation), whereas the latter are involved in the vicious circle (devaluation–inflation–devaluation). Moreover, the French experience confirms that it is very difficult for a weak currency (what we would call, perhaps more appropriately, a 'contestable' currency) to regain credibility, despite disinflation and satisfactory macroeconomic performance (with the exception of unemployment, which is sticky downward).

2. A weak-currency country is exposed to the risk of overvaluation of its real exchange rate, and the negative implications this may have on the price competitiveness of exports and the trade balance. In the EMS, the adjustments of nominal exchange rates have only partly (up to 70 to 80 per cent) offset inflation differentials. Partial adjustment of exchange rates ('partial' if we take purchasing power parity as the benchmark) has induced a bias toward overvaluation of real exchange rates for the weak-currency countries, and conversely, undervaluation of real exchange rates for hard-currency countries. We think that one cause (of course, not the only one) of the recent deterioration of the French trade balance is the loss of price competitiveness resulting from some overvaluation of the French franc.

3. By pegging the French franc to the Deutschmark, French monetary authorities have 'bought' the credibility of the Bundesbank. The price to pay for this could be assessed in terms of interest rate differential, real exchange rates and price competitiveness, lower real growth and so on.

The burden of adjustment Under Bretton Woods, the burden of adjustment primarily fell on deficit countries which had to intervene on foreign exchange markets in order to maintain parity or, if necessary, had to devalue and implement a restrictive economic policy. Countries in surplus were reluctant to revalue and to reflate the economy. The same kind of asymmetry has prevailed in the functioning of the EMS.

Weak-currency countries have had to intervene heavily on foreign exchange markets and to implement restrictive economic policies. No doubt this asymmetry is unavoidable. But it cannot reach a certain threshold without raising economic and political difficulties.

The Nyborg agreements of September 1987 to strengthen the EMS could be interpreted in the following way: let economic policy and international monetary coordination correct, at least partly, the asymmetry between West Germany and its partners within the EMS that comes from the functioning of the market and credibility differential. Before Nyborg, West Germany was in the position of the nth country, which leaves the (n-1) other countries intervening on the foreign exchange market to maintain parity (exactly like the United States under Bretton Woods with the burden of intervention shared by the other countries). The Nyborg package has introduced two important corrections:

— As far as 'intramarginal' interventions (i.e. interventions which keep the parities within the fluctuation margins) are concerned, the burden is split between hard-currency countries (especially Germany) and contestable-currency countries. Intervention by the latter is complemented by active intervention by surplus countries. The asymmetry summarized by the (n-1) argument remains, but it is noticeably reduced.
— New stand-by facilities are granted to deficit countries by countries in surplus.

Until now, the Nyborg package has worked rather efficiently, as the coordinated management of the November 1987 crisis illustrates.

The drop in the dollar created the usual wedge between the French franc and the Deutschmark by putting upward pressure on the German currency. In the face of this, the Bundesbank and the Bank of France implemented, in early November 1987 a coordinated interest rate policy as a substitute for a parity realignment: the increase in French interest rates was concomitant with a significant drop in German rates. The widening of the interest rate differential was, at the time, necessary and sufficient to deter speculation, and avoid a realignment.

Asymmetry in collective preferences Asymmetry lies not only in constraints, but also in preferences. The objective function of

German policy-makers is different from other EMS countries' objective functions: West Germany shows the highest degree of aversion to inflation within the EMS (and ERM) zone, and the collective optimum on the German Phillips' curve corresponds to a combination (inflation–output–unemployment) characterized by a moderate real growth. This bias toward a low inflation–moderate growth solution is reinforced by the well-known demographic constraints: given the demographic structure, a much lower growth is required in West Germany than in France, to keep the rate of unemployment steady or to reduce it to a certain level. Concomitant with the reductions of many intra-European gaps (the inflation gap, the gap concerning the flexibility on domestic labour markets, etc.), the persistent and perhaps growing discrepancy in demographic structure between France and Germany may be one of the most stringent obstacles to a full coordination between the two countries in the next ten years.

France and the anchor for the EMS

Until now, the Deutschmark has been the anchor of the EMS. Will this be the situation in the future? Can we expect the ECU to replace the Deutschmark? Is there a debate between France and Germany on this issue?

Competition between currencies is a major factor in the evolution of the EMS. The ECU remains a 'partial' money (to use Sir John Hicks' term) for many reasons including both the absence of a true European Central Bank and the definition of the European currency. A currency defined as a basket of currencies may have some comparative advantage for the denomination of financial operations in a world of financial instability, since it reduces exchange rate and interest rate risk (see the dramatic growth of the private market for ECU between 1982 and 1986). But a basket is dominated by its contents as far as commercial transactions are concerned: transaction costs remain higher on the basket than on each of the components. The private market for ECU reached a threshold in its development in 1986–7, and to go beyond this threshold it is necessary to introduce significant qualitative changes in the organization of the European currency area. Under 'qualitative changes', we mean at least two modifications:

1. A move towards *direct* definition of the ECU, which would replace the prevalent indirect definition. Instead of being

measured indirectly from the value of the currencies included in the basket, the ECU will be defined directly, and will be the standard for the definition of national currencies. Such a move is conditioned by many changes (like the creation of a European Central Bank, a merging of the official and private circulation of the ECU). It could be seen as necessary, but not a sufficient, condition for the use of the ECU for current transactions (see the argument for transactions costs, p. 85).

2. a clear position concerning the relationship between the ECU (so redefined) and national currencies. We do not think that the ECU, transformed into a 'complete' currency, could remain a parallel currency. The pattern of several complete currencies competing in the same market area could be very unstable, since competition between monies is rarely peaceful and since operators' preferences may induce strong preferences (e.g. lexicographic orders) between them.

On none of these issues has the official position of the French authorities been made clear. So far, French policy-makers, like the Italian authorities, have been keen to promote the use of the ECU (official and private) in its present definition. Nobody can say that we are ready to face the implications of a true European currency, in terms of loss of national monetary sovereignty. As far as the German position is concerned, it is perhaps more clear-cut: the Bundesbank has a preference for a solution close to the status quo. The German Central Bank is reluctant to promote the Deutschmark as the official standard and reserve currency of the zone, and to assume the responsibility attached to this. The Bundesbank, in spite of the official recognition of the domestic use of the ECU (summer 1987), is not favourable to further advances for the European currency in its present definition: strong-currency countries would have to adjust on average policies and performances, perhaps in some cases on the worst. There remains only a third scenario, which corresponds to a new definition of the ECU in relation to the creation of a European Central Bank. Here we come back to the main issue.

From a functional to an institutional approach: France and the European coordination of national monetary policies

France and the Mundell-Padoa Schioppa dilemma From the literature on optimum currency areas initiated by R. Mundell in the early 1960s (and applied to the European case by Padoa-Schioppa), we know that it is impossible to have fixed exchange rates, perfect capital mobility and autonomous monetary policies at the same time. At most, two elements of this 'inconsistency triangle' can be combined. Depending on the combination that prevails, Christian de Boissieu (1988) has distinguished three basic scenarios for the evolution of the EMS.

The *fully cooperative scenario*. International coordination makes fixed exchange rates and perfect capital mobility consistent. Of course convergence in economic performance would alleviate the task of coordination. But this condition goes beyond the reduction in inflation gaps; it also involves considerations of external balances (the issue of structural deficits and surpluses within the EC), the flexibility on the labour market, the industrial structures, and so on. At some point, the fully cooperative scenario would imply new institutional steps, such as the creation of a European central bank or a new definition for the ECU.

Partial coordination. In this scenario, some EC member countries would be tempted to keep some divergences *vis-à-vis* the most virtuous countries, by resorting to some kind of reregulation (such as safeguard clauses) in case of necessity or by requiring a wider margin for their currency in the exchange rate mechanism of the EMS.

The *non-cooperative scenario*. Some member countries would leave the ERM of the EMS, in order to keep some autonomy for their monetary policy under perfect capital mobility (a generalization of the combination adopted by the UK).

Christian de Boissieu has elsewhere (1988) tackled the normative issues (which scenario is the best for each country, for the EC zone, for the world?) and the positive aspects (which scenario is the most likely?). European integration has not yet reached a point where, given the existing conflicts of interest, one can be confident that the fully cooperative scenario will prevail.

French monetary authorities favour this cooperative scenario. The 1982–3 debate on France's membership of the ERM has receded. Given disinflation and the adjustment to the German rate of inflation, and the economic outlook, there is no prospect, in either the short or the medium run, for the use by France of the safeguard clauses or for the reregulation of capital flows.

France and the implementation of the Delors Report The report on *Economic and Monetary Union in the European Community* was presented by a special committee appointed at the Hanover

European Summit (June 1988) and chaired by Jacques Delors. This report proposes a three-stage integration process leading to irrevocably fixed exchange rates and implying major institutional steps (such as creation of a European System of Central Banks (ESCB), and new procedures for the coordination of fiscal policies.

The gradualism embedded in the scheme proposed by the Delors Report is unavoidable, since a 'big bang' approach to the sensitive issue of monetary sovereignty seems out of the question for political reasons. But gradualism may also lead to interrupted progress, to regrets and retreats. As already pointed out, we are still exposed to a deregulation–reregulation cycle.

French authorities have globally endorsed the sequence of events corresponding to the three-stage approach. Nevertheless, some aspects deserve more attention.

There is a pending conflict of interest between strong-currency countries and contestable-currency countries about the creation of a European Central Bank, its rules of functioning, and its role. For France, the major exogenous variable is German monetary policy. A European Central Bank would be a means of internalizing a part of the external constraint associated with German monetary policy, especially if decisions are not taken under the rule of unanimity (the 1985 Single European Act has accelerated the passage to the rule of qualified majority). Conversely, for West Germany, a European Central Bank would create a risk in externalizing what has remained until now internal, that is, decisions about the stance of German monetary policy.

The Delors Report has given rise to a lively but muddled debate about the coordination of national fiscal policies. For some experts, fiscal policy will be more autonomous under perfect capital mobility, since deficit countries will be in a position to borrow from abroad. We belong to the other group, and think that, all things considered, the need for fiscal coordination (coming from the harmonization of taxes, the credibility constraint not only on monetary policy but also on budgetary policy, etc.) will override all other aspects.

The scenario of a parallel currency within the EC zone has been rightly discarded by the Delors Report. It remains to propose a new definition and a new perspective for the ECU. France, traditionally favourable to the development of the European currency unit, has here a particular role to fulfil.

How to manage the risk of delocalization: adjustments in the regulatory framework and the tax system

The level of adjustment and the risk of competitive deregulation Competition between regulators may take place at both the domestic and the international level. Competitive deregulation in the EC, resulting from the desire of national authorities to attract funds and activities (offensive strategy) or to avoid an adverse shift in the location of savings (defensive strategy), means in many cases an adjustment on the 'short side' of the market for regulation (the minimum level for taxation; the maximum for deposit interest rates and the application of the clause of the 'least regulated country'. This could improve welfare, but also, in some circumstances, damage stability. A satisfactory trade-off between efficiency and stability implies that in some cases (for example prudential control) the adjustment would not be on the 'short side'.

The deregulation of deposit rates and the new structure of bank revenues In order to avoid the flight of sight and time deposits, France will have to phase out all regulation concerning deposit rates. As far as demand deposits are concerned, Table 3.5 suggests the coexistence of three groups of countries.

Table 3.5. Interest payments on demand deposits
(%: December 1988)

United States	0
France	0
West Germany	0–2 (dominant values: 0.25 and 0.5)
The Netherlands	0.55 (average value)
Belgium	0.50 (average value)
Spain	7.0 (average value)

First, we have a few countries with no explicit interest payments on demand deposits (France, the United States). Second, some countries have had deregulated interest rates for a long time, but the bank cartel and also moral suasion by the central bank explain the low level of deposit rates (for example, West Germany). Lastly, in some southern countries (for example, Spain and Italy) real interest rates on demand deposits are positive, but this is combined with high interest rates on banks' reserves with the central bank. Given the degree of bank concentration and the moral suasion exercised by French monetary authorities and despite the recent and aggressive move by some British banks, we expect France to join the group of West Germany, namely to show modest interest payments on demand deposits ('modest' means deposit rates significantly negative in real terms).

Complete deregulation of deposit rates in France will be one aspect of a package consisting of a radical change in bank revenues. New competitive conditions will impose a quick transition from the present structure (I) in Figure 3.4 to the structure (II), whatever the political environment.

Figure 3.4 Effect of financial liberalization on pricing structure of banks

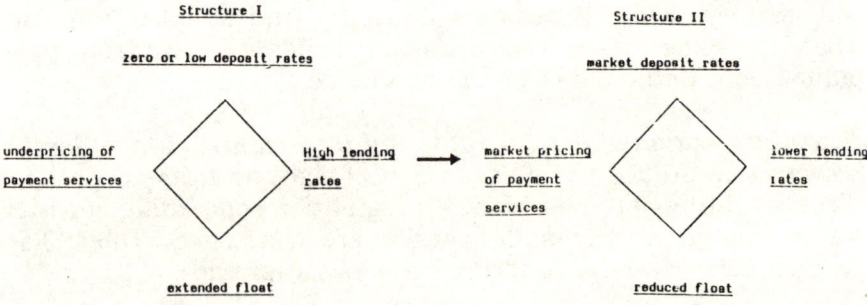

Financial liberalization imposes a dramatic change in the 'magic square' represented in Figure 3.4. French banks could not continue to underprice numerous ancillary and payment services and to overcharge for intermediation operations, since this would make payment services difficult to attract from abroad (inertia effects may be powerful in this case), whilst it is quite certain that overpricing intermediation operations in a world of perfect capital mobility risks the flight of financial activities abroad.

The passage from structure I to structure II, to be socially and politically acceptable, must be *profit-neutral* for the main categories of agents. Globally speaking, the level of net banking income will not be changed, *ceteris paribus*. Only the structure of net banking income will be modified, with a higher proportion of commissions and fees. Likewise, consumers' organizations will accept the move only if it is globally welfare-neutral.

Behind global neutrality, significant *distribution effects* would result from the transition to structure II. The losers of the present combination of underpriced payment services and overpriced intermediation operations (e.g., the small and medium-sized enterprises which have no direct access to disintermediated financing) would be the winners of this structural change.

Adjustments in financial taxation Delocalization of savings and financial activities will depend on compared financial packages rather than on piecemeal comparisons. Individual investors, institutional investors, banks and insurance companies will compare the quality of financial services and the level of return of different financial centres. As usual, taxation is a crucial variable for the determination of comparative advantages.

Official reports, by the Boiteux Committee (1988) and by the Lebègue Committee (1988), have shown that, in order to curb the risk of delocalization, financial taxation has to be adjusted downwards. The adjustment applies to taxes on financial instruments and on financial institutions as well.

Taxation of financial institutions The French banking sector was and still is largely subject to specific taxes: on wages, on the outstanding amount of credit, and so on. This idiosyncratic situation arises from the fact that the extension of value-added tax in 1968 did not apply to the banking sector. Up to now, as far as bank net income is concerned, only commissions and fees are subject to VAT. Removal of the remaining tax idiosyncrasies would require a general application of VAT to banks (or the implementation of a specific tax on French banks which would integrate the piecemeal measures prevailing at present).

Taxes on financial instruments In France, there is a wide range of tax rates on income derived from financial instruments:

— 0 per cent (tax-exempt passbook accounts such as *livrets A* with the Caisses d'épargne and *livrets bleus* with Crédit mutuel);
— 26–7 per cent on bonds;
— 33 per cent on negotiable claims;
— 47 or 52 per cent on non-negotiable savings certificates issued by, for example, banks or the Treasury, depending on the absence or the existence of anonymity.

Moreover, given the corporate income tax rate on distributed profits (42 per cent) and a 50 per cent face value for tax credit, the actual tax credit on dividends (*avoir fiscal*) is equal to 69 per cent, as compared to 100 per cent in West Germany. Most of the distortions have to be corrected by July 1990. Besides the complete removal of the special tax on stock market transactions (*impôt de bourse*), necessary to bring Paris into line with external (especially London) conditions, the French system has to adjust in two ways:

1. The reduction in average and marginal tax rates: this applies to interest rates, dividends, capital gains, and so on. The Lebègue Committee has presented very precise recommendations for the taxation of UCITS (Undertakings for Collective Investment in Transferable Securities), the gradual abolition of discrimination between income and capital gains, and the harmonization of withholding taxes in the EC countries at rates chosen after coordination between member countries. Withholding taxes reduce, or even remove, the tax gap between residents and non-residents, provided that these taxes are not supplemented by other income taxes. This condition will be satisfied if the adjustment is not on the 'short side', but on a rate intermediate between the extreme values (for instance, the withholding tax on bonds, paid in full, may have a rate between the German level (10 per cent until July 1989, 0 per cent after) and the French one (26–7 per cent)). As far as the tax credit on dividends is concerned, we must expect a gradual drop in corporate income tax to 33 per cent (rather than an increase in the face value of tax credit), and the abolition of the discrimination recently introduced between the tax rate on distributed (42 per cent) and retained (39 per cent) profits.

2. Harmonization of control procedures: this is crucial since it clearly affects delocalization of savings and since there are persistent gaps within the EC. For instance, the rather inquisitorial system at work in France is far removed from the German procedure. The very conception of the great internal market implies adjustment on liberal solutions, but not always on the 'short side'. Withholding taxes will constitute in many cases the optimal cooperative solution, since these provide a satisfactory balance between control and liberalism.

The bulk of the adjustment will take place in 1990, and will be integrated in the 1990 budget. The special tax on bank credit was removed in January 1989, and other measures were implemented in 1989 (a more favourable tax rule regarding coupons on UCITS, the removal of the 5.15 per cent tax on life insurance contracts, etc.)

Downward adjustment has to cope with two major constraints:

1. The government fiscal constraint: the calculations made by the Boiteux Committee and the Lebègue Committee indicate a loss of income for the budget close to 30 billion French francs. When added to the drop in taxes caused by a significant downward move of VAT, this represents an impressive figure. Clearly, given the time schedule of deregulation, adjustment in financial taxation will be given first priority. But the fiscal constraint on the French government is tight and will be tighter in case of a slowdown in real growth. Accordingly, the authorities will have to compensate for the reduction of financial taxation (perhaps by broadening the income tax base or by other means).

2. General political constraint: it is difficult for any government to alleviate the taxation of capital income while implementing a relatively stringent control over taxation of labour incomes and the growth of real wages.

Adjustment in quasi-taxes Any banking regulation can formally be interpreted as a tax on the banking sector, without prejudging who will be the final taxpayer (the banks? the depositors, due to lower deposit interest rates? the borrowers, due to higher lending rates?) The set of quasi-taxes is rather heterogeneous, since it includes reserve requirements, deposit insurance schemes and premiums, liquidity ratios, the tax regime for bank provisioning, and so on. However, all these elements of the regulatory framework may induce or speed up some delocalization of financial activities.

Reserve requirements France is in an intermediate situation as far as reserve requirements are concerned. Clearly, some elements of Table 3.6 must be related to the interest payments on demand deposits (for instance, the high deposit rates on demand deposits are, for the banks, partly offset by the high interest rate on compulsory reserves). In most EC countries, as in the USA or in Japan, reserve requirements are no longer an active tool of monetary policy. They are low and seldom changed.

In a world of rapid financial innovation and tough competition between direct financing (disintermediation) and bank financing, monetary authorities could not resort to significant manipulations of the reserve requirement ratio. In this matter, France could remain in an intermediate position provided it

Table 3.6. Reserve requirements (%: December 1988)

		Ratio		Interest payments
		(1)	(2)	
France	demand deposits	5	0	no
	time deposits, savings accounts and related financial instruments	2.5	0	no
Germany	demand deposits	6.6–12.1 (according to size of deposit)	12.1	no
	time deposits	4.95	4.95	no
	savings accounts	4.15	4.15	no
USA	demand deposits and other checkable deposits	3–12 (according to size)	0 (in principle)	no
	time deposits	0–3 (according to maturity)	0 (in principle)	no
Spain	25 % of the variation in the outstanding amount of demand deposits, time deposits and related financial instruments	16.5	0	an interest rate (7.5 %) is paid on a fraction of reserves (11.5 % of the global ratio of 16.5 %).
Italy (1) and (2)	time deposits and CDs	0.125–1.75 (according to size)		5.5 %
Japan (1) and (2)	other deposits	0.25–2.5 (according to size)		no
The UK	no reserve requirements 'a cash ratio deposits scheme' the ratio is equal to 0.45 % of eligible liabilities (0.25 % in some particular cases)			no

(1) residents   (2) non-residents

follows possible adjustments in the main EC countries.

Liquidity ratio In many EC countries there is nothing equivalent to the liquidity ratio implemented in France and altered in February 1988. The purpose of the 1988 reform was to extend the application of the liquidity ratio to all credit institutions (including the *maisons de titres* defined by Article 99 of the 1984 Banking Act), to branches settled abroad, and to all currencies (monitoring is no longer limited to operations in French francs, but also concerns operations in foreign currencies).

Through the moral suasion of the BIS (Bank for International Settlements) and the intervention of the European Economic Commission, it is likely that many European countries (including West Germany) will have to implement a liquidity ratio close to that prevailing in France.

Deposit insurance With enlarged competition and the gradual development of a market for demand and time deposits, the present deposit insurance scheme will have to be adapted. Corresponding to an unfunded and purely contractual regime, it has to be similar to the funded regime in place in most Anglo-Saxon countries (not to speak of risk-based insurance premiums as a way of limiting the well-known 'moral hazard' problem).

Provisioning The law concerning provision on sovereign debt and associated tax deductions is relatively liberal in France, compared to other OECD countries. The attitude of the authorities has favoured the high provisioning ratio of French banks. In this field, there is no need for adjustment in the light of new competitive pressures.

The deregulation of UCITS Despite the 50 per cent market share of French UCITS in total European UCITS, monetary authorities will have to alleviate present rules concerning open-ended unit trusts and mutual funds. For instance, constraints on portfolio management by UCITS, such as the floors and the ceilings concerning the holding of bonds ('*l'obligation de l'obligation*'), have to be removed. It is likely that money-market funds (i.e. funds totally invested in money-market instruments, like those common in the United States will be authorized before long.

Notes

1. The 1945 banking law established a clear-cut classification of credit institutions and banking activities: besides setting up a clear borderline between commercial banks, which can collect demand and short-term deposits, and investment banks, the regulation especially distinguished the average maturity of the credits and the field of intervention (export financing, agriculture, housing, etc.).
2. This expression has been suggested by L. and V. Levy-Garboua (1972).
3. This kind of central bank credit facility has largely supplanted the traditional rediscounting at privileged fixed interest rates. Discount credit on concessional terms is still granted to banks for medium-term export paper, but the rate applied has progressively been raised in relation to market rates. As a consequence, the discount rate has today little impact on interest rates in the interbank market.
4. 'La Banque de France est l'institution qui, dans le cadre de la politique économique et financière de la nation, reçoit de l'Etat la mission générale de veiller sur la monnaie et le crédit. A ce titre, elle veille au bon fonctionnement du système bancaire. Le capital de la Banque de France appartient à l'Etat'.
5. 'Pour le compte de l'Etat et dans le cadre des instructions générales du Ministre de l'Economie et des Finances, la Banque de France régularise les rapports entre le franc et les devises étrangères et gère les réserves publiques de change. Elle peut participer, avec l'autorisation du Ministre d l'Economie et des Finances, à des accords monétaires internationaux'.
6. The new financial environment led French authorities to reform monetary aggregates since the meaning of traditional monetary aggregates has increasingly been questioned. Firstly, the former classification based on an institutional criterion became less and less relevant as the distinction between banks and non-bank institutions became thinner and thinner. Today, all networks tend to offer similar financial services and products. Secondly, the possibility of trading assets (UCITs and short-term mutual funds) presenting sufficient degrees of liquidity and security to substitute for monetary assets and at the same time paying interest, called for a major reviewing of the old borderline between monetary and non-monetary assets. The reform of monetary aggregates took place in 1986 along the following lines: the abandonment of the institutional criterion (as a result, all credit institutions are subject to credit regulation); the need to take into account the fast-growing operations undertaken by the Money Market Mutual Funds, known in France as the Organismes de Placement Collectif en Valeurs Mobilières (OPCVM); a new delimitation of monetary assets according to a functional criterion. On the whole, four aggregates have been defined, M1, M2, M3 and L (liquidities) which can be conveniently compared to those existing in the

United States. M1 comprises notes and coins and demand deposits (including those offered by the OPCVM); M2 comprises M1 plus the saving accounts; M3 is equal to M2 plus time deposits and negotiable certificates of deposit (CDs); L adds to M3 money-market securities.

References

Artus, P. (1987a) 'Asymmetries in the European economies and policy coordination', paper presented at the AEA Conference on Monetary and Financial Models (Geneva) 22–3 January.

Artus, P. (1987b) 'La politique monétaire en France', *Revue Française d'Economie* (Summer).

Artus, P., Y. Barroux and J. Pecha (1987) 'Objectif quantitatif de croissance de la masse monétaire et fonction de réaction des autorités monétaires', *Cahiers Economiques et Monétaires* (Bank of France), 27.

Artus, P. and C. de Boissieu (1988) 'The process of financial innovation', in A. Heertje (ed.) *Innovation, Technology and Finance*, Oxford, Basil Blackwell.

de Boissieu, C. (1988) 'Financial liberalization and the evolution of the EMS', *European Economy*, 36 (May).

de Boissieu, C. (1989) 'The French banking sector in the light of European financial integration', Paper presented at the INSEAD conference on European Banking after 1992, 8–10 February.

Boutillier, M. and P. Villa (1985) 'Politique monétaire en economie d'endettement', *Observations et Diagnostics Economiques*, October.

Bruneel, D. (1987a) 'Money market and monetary regulation in France', Paper presented at the 4th Annual Capital Market Conference (Turkey) August.

Bruneel, D. (1987b) 'The reform of the French financial system', Paper presented at the Symposium on The New Financial Systems, organized by the International Foundation for Human Sciences, 8–10 October.

Conseil National du Crédit, *Annual Reports*.

Duprat, M.H. (1988) 'Free capital movements and the European monetary system'; *Tokyo Club Paper 2*, Tokyo Club Foundation for Global Studies.

Giavazzi, F. and A. Giovannini (1988) 'Models of the EMS: is Europe a greater Deutschmark area?', *Revue Economique* 39 (May).

Kneeshaw, J.T. and P. Van den Bergh (1989) 'Changes in central bank money market operating procedures in the 1980s', *BIS Economic Papers*, 23 (January).

Levy-Garboua, L. and V. (1972) 'Le comportement bancaire, le diviseur de crédit et l'efficacité du contrôle monétaire', *Revue Economique*, March.

Mastropasqua, C., S. Micossi and R. Rinaldi (1988) 'Interventions, sterilisation and monetary policy in European Monetary System countries, 1979–87, in Francesco Giavazzi, Stefano Micossi and Marcus Miller (eds) *The European Monetary System*, Cambridge.

Melitz, J., (1985) 'The French financial system: mechanisms and questions of reforms', in J. Melitz and C. Wyplosz (eds.), *The French Economy, Theory and Policy*, Westview Press.

Melitz, J. and P. Michel, (1986) 'The dynamic stability of the European Monetary System', CEPR *Discussion Paper*, No.96.

Oudiz, G. and H. Sterdyniak, (1985) 'Inflation, employment and external constraints: an overview of the French economy during the seventies', in J. Melitz and C. Wyplosz (eds.), *The French Economy, Theory and Policy*, Westview Press.

Ungerer, H., O. Evans, T. Mayer and P. Young (1986): *The European Monetary System: Recent Developments*, International Monetary Fund, Washington, D.C., December.

Wyplosz, C. (1988) 'Monetary policy in France: monetarism or Darwinism?', unpublished manuscript, INSEAD.

4 British monetary policy and European monetary integration

Richard Brown

1 Introduction

This chapter focuses on developments in UK monetary policy, including external aspects, within the context of the movement within the EC to complete the single market programme, commonly known as the '1992 process'. The 1992 process clearly implies growing integration of the intra-European markets in goods and services; in principle it also suggests increasing mobility of capital and labour within Europe. This will change the monetary environment facing member states, pushing them more in the direction of becoming regions within one monetary area as against independent monetary entities. How far this process will go in practice will obviously depend in part on political factors; but the underlying forces are economic and it is these which are examined in this chapter.

The UK position is particularly interesting because, at the time of writing, the UK is not a full member of the European Monetary System (EMS) in the sense that sterling does not participate in the ERM (exchange rate mechanism). Thus the monetary options facing the UK are much wider than for full EMS members. In order to explore these choices we begin by noting the essence of UK macroeconomic developments and policies during the 1960s and 1970s – these are relevant because it was the perceived failure of these policies which led to the adoption of a very different approach by the Conservative government of 1979. The new policy stance was encapsulated in the Medium-Term Financial Strategy (MTFS) of 1980, which is outlined in section 3; this section also notes subsequent developments in fiscal policy, which is an important influence on monetary policy. This clears the decks for a much closer examination of monetary and exchange rate policy during the 1980s in section 4. We begin by examining the objectives of monetary policy – both as stated by the monetary authorities and as they seem to have evolved in practice. Next, we look at how monetary policy has been implemented. We then consider exchange rate policy and external influences on monetary policy; this leads naturally to a discussion of the participation of sterling in the process of global macroeconomic policy coordination (the Plaza-Louvre process), which began once the policy of benign neglect of the dollar was abandoned in 1985. Section 4 concludes with a review of institutional influences on UK monetary policy.

One common development affecting monetary policy in all countries has been the growing integration of the world economy, especially, during the 1980s, with respect to financial flows. Section 5 surveys how the UK economy has fared in this respect, distinguishing between European and non-European influences, and speculates on some possible consequences of the 1992 process. Section 6 reviews attitudes within the UK towards European monetary integration, including the vexed issue of full sterling participation in the ERM. Finally Section 7 draws together some conclusions.

2   British macroeconomic performance and policies in the 1960s and 1970s

During this period the fundamental objective of British macroeconomic policy, which was agreed by all political parties, was to maintain aggregate demand at a level which minimized unemployment. In principle this involved manipulating Keynesian policy tools such as the level of government spending, taxes and interest rates, so as to boost demand when unemployment was above what would now be regarded as a very low level. In practise such fine-tuning was subject to constraints, in particular the balance of payments and inflation; at times these constraints prevented aggregate demand from being raised to a level considered desirable on strict employment grounds.

Under this regime monetary policy was very much a subsidiary policy instrument, at least until the mid-1970s.

When unconstrained, its intermediate objective was the achievement of low interest rates to boost industrial investment; consumer credit controls, intended to maximize the flow of credit to favoured sectors, were also a feature. Until the collapse of the Bretton Woods system in 1971 the maintenance of a fixed exchange rate meant that excess demand pressure in the UK manifested itself more in the form of a balance of payments deficit than in a significant rise in inflation; the usual monetary policy response to such pressure was to raise short-term interest rates in order to moderate capital outflows and to help deflate demand. Prices and incomes policies were the main anti-inflation tool, though their use was intermittent.

Table 4.1. Average annual changes in key UK economic aggregates,%

	1950–9	1960–9	1970–9	1980–8
GDP	2.5	3.3	2.2	2.2
Consumer prices	13.7	3.4	12.6	7.6
Unemployment (%)	1.5	2.2	3.7	10.3

Sources: GDP – Central Statistical Office *UK National Accounts*, 1989 edition (constant factor cost, average estimate); Consumer prices – IMF International Financial Statistics, various editions; Unemployment – OECD Main Economic Indicators.

In general, macroeconomic policy during the 1950s and 1960s succeeded in keeping unemployment low while inflation rarely exceeded 5 per cent. Nevertheless the average growth rate of GNP, at just under 3 per cent, was regarded as unsatisfactory and several abortive attempts at industrial planning were made to try to increase it. Furthermore, unemployment was tending to rise towards the end of the 1960s. With the benefit of hindsight this reflected more the failure of supply rather than demand, to grow as fast as hoped, especially as inflation was also creeping up. Nevertheless in 1971 the Conservative government adopted expansionary fiscal and monetary policies in a 'dash for growth' and sterling was floated in June 1972 to ease the external constraint. Growth did indeed pick up but inflation, boosted by the worldwide explosion of primary product prices, rose dramatically, peaking at over 25 per cent in the mid-1970s. The Labour government of 1974 tried to follow Keynesian policies in the face of severe inflation and external constraints. These, however, weakened external confidence to the extent that the government had to agree to an IMF financial programme in 1976 following a collapse of confidence in sterling. Though the programme was basically adhered to, the attempt to impose a series of incomes policies led to increasing industrial disputes and contributed to the Conservative election victory of 1979.

3   The medium-term financial strategy

During the 1980s British macroeconomic policy has in principle been determined in accordance with the Medium-Term Financial Strategy (MTFS) introduced by the Conservative government shortly after it came to power in June 1979. The content and emphasis of the MTFS was greatly influenced by the macroeconomic experiences of the 1970s and, in particular, by the monetarist interpretation of the perceived failure of macroeconomic policy over this period. This interpretation included:

— the strong belief that high and variable inflation was a major constraint on growth; the earlier view that there could be a positive trade-off between inflation and growth, such that more growth could be 'bought' at the expense of some increase in inflation, was decisively rejected – the new view was that low inflation was a prerequisite for the restoration of sustainable growth.
— the complete rejection of prices and incomes policies as a way of controlling inflation; these policies were regarded as ineffectual in achieving their main aim and indeed as counterproductive in that the associated microeconomic distortions hindered growth.
— the belief that inflation was a monetary phenomenon which could be controlled by a sufficiently tight monetary policy, especially if such a policy was publicly announced.
— the view that such a monetary policy itself required strict control of the public-sector financial deficit.

The 1970s were also felt to have important lessons for the achievement of sustainable growth at a satisfactory rate. The essential philosophy was that growth sprang from the private sector. In order for this to be realized, however, certain preconditions had to be achieved:

— the public sector, which was inherently inefficient, had to be reduced in size to release resources for use in the more productive private sector;
— the various controls which had increasingly been put on the private sector had to be lifted, and the high marginal direct tax rates had to be cut to encourage enterprise;
— the power of the trade unions had to be significantly curbed.

This reappraisal implied a radical change in the thrust of economic policy. Indeed Nigel Lawson, who as the then Financial Secretary was one of the principal architects of the MTFS, claimed in his Mais lecture of June 1984 that the thrust had been reversed. Previously macroeconomic policy had been assigned the achievement of full employment (via demand management) while the control of inflation was the responsibility of microeconomic policy (prices and incomes policies etc.); now the control of inflation was the responsibility of macroeconomic policy while microeconomic policy would achieve the creation of conditions conducive to growth and employment.

The original MTFS appeared with the budget of March 1980. Although the fiscal and monetary projections associated with the MTFS have been revised in subsequent budgets, government ministers have repeatedly claimed that their macroeconomic policy decisions have been consistent with the spirit of the original MTFS and, indeed, that the strategy has always been on course. We will investigate later whether such claims are justified. Let us first note the key features of the MTFS:

— as anticipated the primary objective of macroeconomic policy became the defeat of inflation;
— towards this end monetary targets were given a central role on the assumption that there was a stable relationship between the demand for money and its determinants, including prices, and that the money supply was under the control of the authorities;
— an implication of this was that interest rates would be raised to whatever level was necessary to bring monetary growth within the target range;
— in order to prevent undue pressure on interest rates from public-sector credit demands, a declining profile for the Public Sector Borrowing Requirement (PSBR) was set out (the links between monetary growth and the PSBR will be elaborated on later);

— although this was not made explicit, a key feature of the MTFS was its insular nature, with very little reference being made to external factors; one corollary was that sterling was free to find its own level on the assumption that as a result external factors would not prejudice the achievement of domestic monetary objectives;

— the emphasis was very much on the medium-term nature of the strategy, eschewing fine-tuning; an important influence here was the rational expectations revolution in economics which, *inter alia*, stressed the importance of *announcing* monetary targets so that economic behaviour could adapt immediately to the new regime, thereby minimizing any loss of output associated with tight policies.

With reference to the last point the essence of the MTFS was encapsulated in published targets for both the PSBR and a measure of the money supply, £M3:

Table 4.2. Original MTFS targets

	PSBR/GDP ratio	Growth of £M3(%)
1980–1	3.75	7–11
1981–2	3.00	6–10
1982–3	2.25	5–9
1983–4	1.5	4–8

The choice of the PSBR as the fiscal target was not controversial, but that of £M3 was less clear cut. £M3 is a measure of broad money which comprises notes and coins and all UK private-sector sterling deposits held in UK banks. Some monetarists argued for a narrower definition of money to be targeted while others wanted several monetary aggregates as targets. However, the monetary authorities then felt that more than one targeted aggregate would be confusing. The preference for £M3 reflected econometric evidence that the demand for £M3 was at least as stable as that for other aggregates. Furthermore £M3 is linked to the PSBR – the increase in £M3 equals the increase in credit to the private and public sectors and net external flows; the increase in credit to the public sector in turn is the amount of the PSBR which is not financed by sales of government securities to the private sector. Thus the use of £M3 enabled the fiscal and monetary targets of the government to be projected on a consistent basis. Finally, and partly for the previous two reasons, £M3 was the only monetary aggregate to have been used as a target before and hence had the benefit of some familiarity.

The development of monetary policy under the MTFS will be examined in detail in the next section. Before that we will briefly note the evolution of fiscal policy, which can be an important constraint on monetary policy. During the first half of the 1980s both the PSBR projections contained in the initial MTFS and the revisions in subsequent budgets were overshot. To a large extent the problem occurred right at the beginning – the severity of the recession in the early 1980s boosted social security spending by much more than expected and this, together with some slippage from other spending targets, led to the PSBR overshoots. However, despite the recession, the move of the current account into surplus and the sharp appreciation of sterling, no attempt was made to ease the tight fiscal stance. After the mid-1980s the PSBR moved into surplus, the size of which increased dramatically after 1986. This partly reflected receipts from the sales of public-sector corporations to the private sector (privatization); a sustained growth in tax revenue once the recovery began and continued restraint on government spending were contributory factors.

The PSBR overshoots in the early years of the MTFS necessitated higher sales of government stock and hence interest rates than would otherwise have been the case. Aside from this it is difficult to argue that the conduct of fiscal policy has posed any great problems for monetary policy in the UK over this period. On the contrary, the large fiscal surpluses and associated redemptions of government stock helped keep long-term interest rates lower than they would otherwise have been in 1988–9 in the face of a deterioration in the inflationary outlook. Indeed the more significant causality may have been the other way round in that the lax monetary policy from the mid-1980s onwards helped fuel the growth of consumer spending and hence tax receipts.

4 The evolution of monetary and exchange rate policy during the 1980s

The objectives of monetary policy

We have already seen that the control of inflation became the primary objective of macroeconomic, and in particular monetary, policy during the 1980s. But what exactly does this mean? Were any targets achieved? If not, was this because the underlying inflationary problem was more severe than anticipated or was the government diverted by the pursuit of other objectives?

There are at least two ways of evaluating a government's inflation objective. The first is to study public statements on the grounds that these reveal what the government wants as against what it gets. The latter is to some extent outside the government's control – for example rises in primary product prices or a substantial appreciation of the US dollar can frustrate the domestic anti-inflation struggle. The counter-argument is that in practice governments have incentives for inflation to turn out somewhat above their stated target – typically governments have substantial net debt, the real value of which is reduced by inflation, and financial policies which are more expansionary than expected can boost output and employment over the all-important (from an electoral point of view) short run. This suggests a second way of evaluating an inflation objective, namely to examine the actual inflation record of the government.

We shall use both criteria in evaluating the inflation objectives of the UK government of the 1980s. This period naturally divides into two – the first, from 1979 to 1983, covers the decline in inflation to under 5 per cent p.a.; the second, from 1983 on, is the interesting period when the government in principle had the opportunity of going for a stable price level but instead opted for encouraging the economic recovery.

Until the mid-1980s the Conservative government had no explicit inflation objective. This was not too surprising because inflation had been high and volatile during the 1970s – by 1979 inflation (annual change in the Retail Price Index) was below the very high rates of the mid-1970s but it was still some 10 per cent and tending to rise. However, in numerous statements made both in opposition and shortly after taking office, the government made it perfectly clear that its target was a sustained reduction in inflation. In the original MTFS this objective is summarized as 'to bring down the rate of inflation and to create conditions for a sustainable growth of output and employment'.

In the event inflation continued rising, peaking at over 20 per cent for a brief period in 1980. As £M3 was also exceeding its target range it is tempting to conclude that the government was not especially determined to control inflation. However, a series of exceptional factors were driving both the RPI and £M3 much higher than expected. Shortly after taking office the government had honoured an election commitment to raise public-sector wages substantially and in its first budget had raised the general VAT rate from 8 per cent to 15 per cent in order to finance a cut in direct taxes; fiscal and efficiency considerations also necessitated substantial increases in public corporation charges. All this took place in the aftermath of the second oil shock and a rebound in private-sector wages following the end of three years of incomes policy. On the monetary front, private-sector credit demand was boosted both by distress borrowing from the industrial sector, as a reaction to a severe recession, and by the ending of controls on banks which penalized excessive growth in bank deposits.

More generally, other monetary indicators suggest that policy was actually tight over this period. Other monetary aggregates were growing less fast than £M3, sterling was very strong, interest rates were high and there was no indication from the movement of house or other asset prices that policy was lax. An even tighter monetary policy would have exacerbated the severe recession which had begun. On balance this episode illustrates more the naivety of those who thought that the mere announcement of monetary targets would bring inflation under control rather than a lack of anti-inflationary resolve on the part of the government. Indeed, once it had peaked inflation fell without interruption, reflecting *inter alia* the tight policy stance and the world recession, and the annual increase in the RPI edged below 5 per cent in 1983.

The second relevant period for analysing the government's inflation objective is from 1983 onwards. Whereas there were good reasons for not having an explicit inflation target under the conditions of the late 1970s, these objections were much less forceful once inflation had fallen to a low figure. At that point the choice was fairly clear cut – either to press ahead and achieve a basically stable aggregate price level or to tolerate a 'low' inflation figure of the order of 3–5 per cent. The government was increasingly urged to make its intentions clear, not least because with continued overshooting of monetary targets and with other factors such as the exchange rate and the state of the real economy appearing to have some influence on policy, there was growing confusion about monetary policy. In response the 1984 budget stated that the government's 'ultimate objective' was the achievement of 'stable prices with lower interest rates'. This ultimate objective of stable prices has been confirmed on several occasions; however, no timetable has ever been set for its achievement.

These circumstances suggest that we should also scrutinize the government's actual inflation record post-1983, especially since, partly because the world macroeconomic environment has become more settled, 'exogenous' influences on inflation have become less important. There is little in the actual record to suggest that the government has given any serious weight to achieving a stable price level. The annual increase in the RPI has averaged some 5 per cent with upward blips occurring in 1985 and, more importantly, from 1988 onwards. The government reacted to these blips by raising short-term interest rates substantially, indicating that it certainly did not want to see inflation above 5 per cent. When inflationary pressure has been subdued, however, short-term interest rates have been pushed downwards, especially if sterling has been subject to upward pressure, despite continued overshooting of monetary aggregates and a massive surge in lending to the personal sector. Furthermore, in the wake of the worldwide collapse of stock markets in October 1987 the UK cut interest rates along with other countries in the (with the benefit of hindsight, mistaken) belief that the recovery might be aborted. All this does not imply that the government did not want to see stable prices actually achieved – but it does suggest that providing inflation did not exceed 5 per cent it gave priority to ensuring that the recovery continued. This verdict would appear to have been reached by the financial markets too, as the yields on long-term government stock have rarely fallen below 9 per cent over this period, indicating an expected inflation rate of at least some 4–5 per cent.

All this said, it is possible that the 1988–9 upturn in inflation will have such an impact on government thinking that short-term interest rates, and the exchange rate, will be held at whatever level is necessary to achieve stable prices and that once achieved this target will not be abandoned – but this possibility is for the moment pure conjecture.

The operation of monetary policy

Thus in the early 1980s the government gave very high priority to bringing down inflation but once this had reached some 5 per cent priority was switched to supporting the recovery rather than achieving stable prices. We now examine how the way in which the government has sought to achieve its monetary objectives has also undergone significant change, such that there is little of the spirit of the original MTFS left. Although any such division is to some extent abitrary, we will recognize three sub-periods:

— 1980–2, the period of trying to adhere to the original MTFS;
— 1982–5, the period of searching for more reliable monetary targets;
— 1985 on, the *de facto* abandonment of monetary targets, with inflation becoming the judge and jury of monetary policy.

We noted earlier that up to the 1970s the essential aim of monetary policy was the maintenance of low interest rates, subject to the need to maintain the fixed exchange rate; the quantitative control of bank lending to the private sector was an important policy instrument. The explosion of inflation in the mid-1970s forced the Labour government, under the urging of the Bank of England and, later, the IMF, to adopt monetary targets but this was very much under duress, with the control of inflation still the responsibility of prices and incomes policy. That said, when confidence was restored in sterling following the IMF agreement of 1976 and the subsequent inflows forced a choice between keeping the exchange rate or the monetary targets, it was the exchange rate target which was abandoned.

1980–2. The original MTFS had strong implications for the methods of monetary control. The adoption of a £M3 target, which was the centrepiece of the government's anti-inflation and macroeconomic policy, carried with it the explicit assumption that interest rates would be free to adjust to whatever level was necessary to achieve the monetary target. The hope was that the publication of a series of monetary targets would defuse inflationary expectations while the phased reduction of the PSBR would reduce real interest rates, so that nominal interest rates would soon fall to relatively low levels; meanwhile the view was that any attempt to keep interest rates artificially low (for example for industrial reasons) would be counterproductive, as the damaging implications for inflationary expectations would soon force up market interest rates.

The implications for the exchange rate were more implicit but the message was similar – the absolute primacy of the monetary target meant that the exchange rate had to be free to adjust to find its own level. Partly this reflected the belief that official intervention in the foreign exchange markets – like interference with any market – would be counterproductive; indeed, shortly after coming to power, the Conservative government abandoned exchange controls. More important was the experience of the UK over 1977–8 (and of Germany over several periods) that significant foreign exchange market intervention could prejudice the achievement of monetary targets, so if the latter were sacrosanct there was no room for the former (with the exception of limited intervention aimed at smoothing erratic market movements).

The general distaste for controls allied with the belief in the virtues of the market mechanism had a further implication for monetary control, namely that there was no room for moral suasion or quantitative controls on credit. In fact, the onward march of financial deregulation and innovation, and the increasingly competitive market for financial services, meant that in any case it was becoming more difficult to impose such controls successfully. Thus in June 1980 the 'corset', or the scheme which imposed penalties on banks if deposits with them expanded beyond a certain rate, was abolished. Later, in July 1982, all official hire-purchase controls were removed.

In essence, then, the initial monetary strategy was to influence short-term interest rates so as to bring £M3 within its target range, irrespective of the exchange rate or of the state of the real economy. In practice the pure version of the MTFS was stillborn. As we have seen, both inflation and the growth of £M3 were independently subject to powerful upward pressures such that £M3 increased by 19.4 per cent over the first target period (cf. a target range of 7–11 per cent) and by 12.8 per cent in the second (cf. a target of 6–10 per cent) despite the fact that there was no attempt to offset the excess monetary growth of the first period. However the importance attached to the MTFS as a means of influencing expectations meant that the monetary overshoot was taken very seriously and it was only the fact that virtually every other indicator, both monetary and non-monetary, was consistent with very tight policy that short-term interest rates were not raised even further.

1982–5. By 1982 it was clear that inflation was well established on a downward path but £M3 was still overshooting. This strengthened the hand of those who argued that £M3 was being affected by the structural changes going on in the financial sector and hence was giving a misleading reading of the monetary picture. At this stage there was no question of dropping £M3 as a target variable – far too much political capital had been invested in stressing its relevance to the fight against inflation. Instead much work was done by the Bank of England and the Treasury on trying to find monetary aggregates which were less distorted. Compared with £M3, both narrower and broader measures were considered. Some monetarists argued for using base money (cash and banks' balances with the Bank of England) on the grounds that this showed a very good statistical relationship with inflation; others, including the Bank of England, felt that the relationship was at best contemporaneous rather than one of changes in base money leading changes in prices. Other monetarists argued for very broad measures of money on the grounds that these would be much less affected by shifts between different financial assets.

The reaction of the monetary authorities in the 1982 budget was to retain £M3 as a target variable but to add both a narrower aggregate, M1, and a broader aggregate, PSL2. All three aggregates had the same target growth range which, at 8–12 per cent, was 3 percentage points above that envisaged for 1982–3 in the original MTFS. At the same time the authorities made it clear that in assessing monetary conditions the behaviour of a wide range of indicators would be taken into account, including the exchange rate. These three aggregates were retained as target variables in the 1983 budget with a common range of 7–11 per cent. But the growth of M1 and PSL2 exceeded this range; this and other problems of interpretation triggered a review of the MTFS in the summer of 1983 under the new Chancellor, Nigel Lawson. The result was a continuation of monetary targets but with M1 and PSL2 dropped and M0 (the monetary base) given equal weight with £M3 in both the 1984 and 1985 budgets. Nevertheless the growth of £M3 continued to exceed its target range and the City was not impressed by the slow growth of M0, which it regarded as a lagging indicator of inflation. At the same time the surge in consumer credit was a fresh cause for concern.

1985 on. This period covers the *de facto* abandonment of monetary targeting in the UK. The abandonment reflects the failure to find a monetary aggregate which was both sufficiently stable and which was felt to be of economic significance by financial markets. Trends in monetary and credit aggregates seemed to have little independent influence on policy – certainly a massive growth in consumer credit was tolerated. The use of £M3 as a target variable was suspended towards the end of 1985 and, when it was reinstated, the target range was a relatively high 11–15 per cent (this was nevertheless exceeded). The Bank of England rationalized the continued high growth of £M3 as representing a permanent build-up of savings by the private sector following changes in the structure of financial intermediation (in particular enhanced competition and the abandonment of controls). The problem with this sort of rationalization is that, unless it is clearly stated in advance of the changes taking effect (which it certainly wasn't, to judge by the earlier £M3 growth ranges) it can be used to excuse any monetary growth rate. The markets were therefore left with MO as the only monetary target but, to quote from the Midland Bank *Review* of autumn 1987 'As a leading indicator of policy it can hardly be taken seriously ... the notion that the small change of the financial system will drive economic activity in general lacks credibility'.

At the same time there was unease that lower interest rates had become an objective in their own right, much as they had been during the Keynesian period of policy-making. Indeed this had been presaged in the 1984 Budget statement, and the government had been embarrassed that interest rates had not fallen as low as might have been expected given the avowed pursuit of responsible financial policies. In the face of growing criticism of the MTFS and of confusion over its monetary objectives, the government emphasized that what really mattered was the inflation rate itself – Nigel Lawson referred to it as the 'judge and jury' of monetary policy. The priority became to encourage economic recovery subject to inflation not exceeding some 5 per cent – when this occurred, as in 1985 and 1988–9, then short-term interest rates were raised sharply. Increasingly, however, the exchange rate was playing a more prominent role in monetary policy.

Developments in exchange rate policy

In a period when exchange rates between the major currencies have undergone massive change, the definition of the sterling exchange rate is not unambiguous. Three definitions have been relevant to policy-making. First, there is the sterling–dollar rate. This is a familiar rate partly because the dollar was the denominator of the Bretton Woods system; the dollar remains the most important currency in world trade and, with a significant proportion of traded goods being denominated in dollars, movements in the dollar rate can be particularly relevant to short-term inflation developments. The effective exchange rate, or the weighted average change in sterling against a basket of currencies, is another important concept – the UK authorities use weights derived from the IMF Multilateral Exchange Rate Model (MERM). The third relevant rate is the sterling–Deutschmark rate because the Deutschmark is the linchpin of the EMS.

Since June 1972 sterling has been floating, though the official influence on the market has varied widely, from benign neglect to fairly active management of the rate. During the 1970s the usual objective was to ensure that sterling did not become uncompetitive – since the UK's inflation rate was above that of most other industrial countries this implied depreciation, with which the market was normally happy to oblige. As concern over inflation grew, however, attitudes towards the exchange rate changed. The policy of 'depreciation to maintain competitiveness' was seen as encouraging inflation, as a strong wage–price spiral quickly reacted to an increase in traded goods prices consequent upon depreciation. Indeed the virtues of a 'high' exchange rate policy were propounded on the grounds that with appreciation the strong wage–price spiral would work to minimize competitiveness losses and maximize the gains from lower than otherwise inflation; meanwhile any losses in competitiveness would encourage industry to trade up and become more efficient (the cold bath theory). It was partly on these grounds that sterling was allowed to float upwards over 1977–8.

The new Conservative government accepted these arguments. However, as we saw earlier, the overriding priority attached to the monetary target in the original MTFS, coupled with a prejudice against intervening in the foreign exchange markets, initially produced a policy of benign neglect to sterling. Consistent with this the government also rejected sterling participation in the ERM of the EMS. Aside from the constraint on the ability to pursue an independent monetary policy, the authorities were also concerned that sharp changes in oil prices would have a strong differential impact on sterling as against other EMS currencies, making frequent adjustments of the sterling–ECU parity necessary.

From an early stage the MTFS envisaged that sterling would

be one of the indicators against which monetary conditions would be judged. An example of this was the 1979–80 period when sterling appreciated strongly, reflecting confidence in the tight financial policies being pursued and the UK's position as an oil exporter at a time of very high oil prices. With domestic prices and costs continuing to rise faster than elsewhere, a massive loss of competitiveness resulted. The consequent impact on industry was one factor which persuaded the authorities not to raise interest rates further despite £M3 overshooting its target.

However, it was not long before sterling became a target in its own right, although the actual target level frequently changed and was rarely clear. For example, by 1981 sterling was tending to depreciate, especially against the strong dollar. The authorities became concerned with the pace of the decline and raised short-term interest rates as a result. To quote from the Bank of England's *Quarterly Bulletin* of December 1981:

the authorities were concerned that a further fall in the exchange rate, following the decline that had already taken place earlier in the year, would have serious adverse implications for inflation. Failure to respond rapidly to downward pressure on sterling appeared likely to risk accelerating sterling's fall, and a rise in the general level of short term interest rates therefore seemed appropriate.

This general situation was repeated on several occasions. Indeed a sort of cycle developed, with periods of upward pressure on sterling allowing falls in UK interest rates to take place, followed by bouts of market anxiety over monetary and/or inflation trends triggering downward pressure on sterling and forcing the authorities to raise short-term interest rates, often sharply. For example,

— in November 1982 bank base rates rose from 9 per cent to 11 per cent as sterling came under heavy pressure;
— in July 1984 these interest rates rose from 9.25 per cent to 12 per cent (partly reflecting a rise in US rates);
— in January 1985 monetary worries, fears about an oil price collapse and the rampant US dollar forced a rise in UK base rates from 9.5 per cent to 14 per cent;
— over 1988–9 concern over the deteriorating inflationary situation and the consequent need to keep up the value of

sterling resulted in a long-drawn-out rise in base rates from 7.5 per cent to 15 per cent (by October 1989).

In between these crisis phases attempts have been made to keep sterling fairly stable – during 1985 the authorities appeared to be trying to keep sterling's effective rate within a range of 78–82; during 1987 and the early part of 1988 a target of DM3 seemed to exist. Indeed with the collapse of monetary targets the exchange rate became the main intermediate monetary objective of the authorities, the target either being to support the recovery, as in 1987/early 1988, or to moderate inflation, as since. Consistent with this, intervention has at times been much heavier than would be implied by mere smoothing operations.

Sterling and the Plaza-Louvre process

Not surprisingly, given the relatively open nature of the economy, the UK has long had an interest in international policy coordination. Arguably the participation of sterling in the Bretton Woods fixed exchange rate system was an example of policy coordination in the sense that macroeconomic policy had to be geared to supporting sterling. After the first oil shock of 1973–4 the then Labour government actively supported efforts to get agreement that the major oil-importing economies should not attempt to deflate away their oil deficits. The UK participated in the Bonn Economic Summit package in 1978 when Germany and Japan agreed to reflate their economies in return for the US adopting energy conservation measures.

Policy coordination was at a low ebb, both in the UK and elsewhere, in the early 1980s when insular monetarism was the vogue. However the experiences of that period have been very relevant in shaping UK attitudes to coordination. In particular the very high level of US interest rates and the strong appreciation of the dollar were widely regarded as detrimental to the UK economy in the sense of forcing UK interest rates above levels warranted on domestic grounds (this is not obvious given the monetary overshooting of the time) and exacerbating imported inflation. Subsequently criticism focused on the unsustainability of US policies and the costs of gross misalignments of exchange rates. As regards the latter, UK experience was also shaped by a reappraisal of the effects of the massive sterling appreciation, which came to be viewed as an important factor behind the depth of the UK recession.

Thus when US policy on the dollar shifted during 1985 the UK willingly participated in the Plaza Agreement. Although no specific policy measures were agreed, the UK joined in subsequent coordinated intervention moves. The UK was also a party to the Louvre Accord of February 1987 which attempted to stabilize the dollar. Although specific policy undertakings were made to back up the Accord, in the UK's case these did not involve any departure from existing policy. In late 1987 the Bank of England cut interest rates as part of a coordinated response to the collapse of world stock markets in October. Finally, Nigel Lawson publicly supported a move to managed floating, building on the Plaza and Louvre agreements. This would involve the maximum stability of exchange rates (as a form of relative coordination) backed up by a review of indicators relevant to inflation (for example commodity prices), possibly an extension of the Tokyo summit indicators, as a form of absolute coordination. All this would be conducted in a nominal, medium-term framework.

The fact that sterling does not at present participate in the ERM and the possibility that the Louvre process may break down have implications for the type of coordination which may be best for the UK. For example, assume that the policy objective is for sterling to be stable against a basket of currencies. In the absence of effective exchange rate coordination among the G3 (US, Germany and Japan) sterling might be more stable floating between the dollar and the Deutschmark; put another way, if sterling was tied to the Deutschmark it might then be forced into inappropriate movements against the dollar. If avoidance of exchange rate misalignments is the objective, then the first-best outcome could be for sterling to participate in the ERM within the broader context of (albeit looser) exchange rate coordination among the G3. However, the second-best outcome is not necessarily participation in the ERM, irrespective of the G3 situation for a currency with significant trade and financial links outside Europe. This point is returned to in section 5.

Institutional influences on policy

Monetary policy objectives, and the instruments used to achieve them, have changed significantly over time, as has the influence of the Bank of England in the formulation of monetary policy. This helps demonstrate that the ground rules surrounding

British monetary policy are more flexible than in some other countries, for example Germany. In consequence greater weight must be placed on practice as against theory or law.

The Bank of England was nationalized in 1946, although it acted as a central bank for at least one hundred years previously. As a public corporation it is in principle free to manage its own affairs although its own degree of operational freedom is quite limited. At the apex of the Bank is a Court of Directors comprising the governor, the deputy governor, four full-time and several part-time directors; all are prime-ministerial appointments. Although there are no hard and fast rules, the governor tends to be appointed from outside the Bank while the deputy governor and the executive directors have usually spent at least part of their careers within the Bank.

The appointment of the governor is an important decision for the Prime Minister. Traditionally it is made with the tacit approval (or at least without the active disagreement) of the Leader of the Opposition on the understanding that the governor is not replaced when the government changes. However the present governor, Mr Robin Leigh-Pemberton, was appointed without such consultation and it is possible that he could be asked to step down if a Labour government came to power before the end of his term of office. Mr Leigh-Pemberton has a background in local Conservative politics and is an example of the growing politicization of public life in Britain.

The influence of the Bank of England on monetary policy has declined over time. At one time the Bank could change the then principal instrument of monetary policy, bank rate, without reference to the Treasury. Now it is unthinkable that the Bank would take a major initiative on monetary policy without full Treasury (and prime-ministerial) support. The Bank's independence has long been under attack. The postwar Labour governments were suspicious that the Bank was using its role as interpreter of financial markets to keep monetary policy tighter than desired by the government. In the 1980s two new factors have emerged. First, monetary policy has become fully integrated within the government's general economic strategy, thereby reducing the potential for an independent monetary policy. Second, on occasions doubts within government circles have emerged over whether the Bank has been fully behind the government's economic strategy – for example the Bank argued that policy was too tight at the beginning of the MTFS, and the Prime Minister was furious that the Bank underestimated the monetary surge which took place after the 'corset' came off. Nevertheless the Bank still retains influence deriving from its experience in operating monetary and exchange rate policy. Its influence within government will tend to be greater when markets are concerned that policy is too lax.

5   The integration of the British economy within the EC and the global economy

The British economy has traditionally been relatively open. In recent years foreign trade has comprised some 25–30 per cent of GNP (average of exports and imports of goods and services, national accounts basis); the underlying trend is upwards, though in recent years this has been masked by a fall in the price and, more recently, in the volume, of trade in oil. The importance of foreign capital flows has also increased. We have already seen that the exchange rate has an important influence on inflation in the UK; similarly we have noted an example of a major international financial disturbance impacting on financial conditions in the UK (the global stock market collapse of October 1987).

The interesting questions are whether the influence of the EC relative to, for example, the US has increased and what might happen in the future. With respect to foreign trade, some indication of changes in the relative importance of the various economic blocs to the UK may be gained from examination of changes in the weights underlying sterling's effective exchange rate index over time. MERM weights attempt to take account of

Table 4.3. Sterling effective exchange rate weights, based on the pattern of trade in:

	1972	1977	1980
US	32.8	24.6	20.4
EC	40.1	47.5	55.6
(Germany)	(13.1)	(14.1)	(20.0)
Japan	11.5	13.7	8.8
Other	15.6	14.2	15.2

Source: Bank of England *Quarterly Bulletin* (March 1977; March 1981; November 1988).

trade in third markets and are thus more comprehensive than weights based on bilateral trade – the importance of changes in Japanese competitiveness, for example, may be felt much more in third markets than in bilateral trade. A particular set of weights is based on trade flows in a certain year (see Table 4.3).

Clearly, the importance of the EC to the UK's trade position has risen significantly, more or less at the expense of the US. This change has taken place to the extent that the weight for Germany is now virtually as great as that for the US while the EC as a bloc is well over half the total. The 1992 process must imply that these trends will continue; any 'Fortress Europe' effect would accelerate them, albeit for unfortunate reasons.

The above relates to trade in goods and services. It is more difficult to get data on capital flows which differentiate the EC portion. The UK's balance of payments data publication has one section which separates out net direct and portfolio flows to the EC. A comparison with the aggregate of such flows seems to confirm a trend similar to that for goods and services. However, capital flows are often dominated in magnitude by banking and other investment flows. Here it is very difficult to get any data on EC aspects. Of some interest here are the attempts of the Bank of England to model the sterling exchange rate. For a period Deutschmark interest rates entered the final equation as a separate variable but they are not distinguished now. However, this may not reflect any diminution of Deutschmark influence on sterling but rather the fact that if interest parity holds between the major currencies then all the major non-sterling interest rates would be directly substitutable in such equations, implying that the use of more than one foreign interest rate would be redundant. The issue then becomes the influence of Deutschmark interest rates on, for example, dollar interest rates.

It might be useful to speculate on how the 1992 process will affect the degree of monetary union within the EC and, of particular relevance to the UK, the balance of economic arguments relating to whether ERM membership, and indeed a subsequent tightening of ERM bands, would be advantageous. The classic advantages of monetary union include the enhanced usefulness of money arising from a reduction of exchange rate volatility, the elimination of speculative capital flows between members of the union (assuming absolutely fixed rates/one currency) and a saving of foreign exchange reserves. The main cost is the loss of the exchange rate as a tool of adjustment, with possible detrimental effects on internal balance, especially in less favoured regions. The issue then becomes how the 1992 process may affect the factors which have an impact on these criteria.

With respect to the use of the exchange rate as a policy tool, recent years have seen a change in emphasis away from using the exchange rate as a competitiveness tool and towards using it as an anti-inflation weapon. This reflects *inter alia* the greater emphasis on fighting inflation, some reduction in competitiveness elasticities and a perceived tightening of the wage–price spiral. It is not so obvious how the 1992 process affects these arguments. For example, though it may be less important to change the sterling exchange rate for competitiveness reasons, some in the UK regard it as a key weapon in the anti-inflation struggle; alternatively they would argue that a fixed exchange rate could prejudice the anti-inflation struggle. However, others in Europe might argue that under these circumstances the UK would be reducing its inflation by exporting it to others and that the UK should tackle its inflation problem at source. What does seem beyond doubt is that when it comes to the definition of the exchange rate then the 1992 process implies a further increase in the importance of EC partners in exchange rate weights.

Other factors impinge on the consequences of losing the exchange rate as a policy tool. For example, an increase in labour mobility, such as is implied by the 1992 process, might reduce some of the regional consequences of a fixed rate; however, it is far from clear how much labour mobility will increase in practice. The degree of openness of European economies should increase further – other things being equal this implies that proportionately smaller changes in demand are needed to correct a given trade imbalance and hence that the costs of giving up the exchange rate as a policy instrument become less important.

Another key criterion is the extent and source of external (to Europe) disturbances. For example, with frequent oil shocks a country which attaches great importance to its inflation objective may well want to retain some flexibility in its exchange rate. Here one might hazard the guess that in general such shocks may be less important in the 1990s than they were in the 1970s or early 1980s, for example: macroeconomic policy is more settled among economies and there is some evidence of increasing consumption and production elasticities, certainly among primary products.

6   Attitudes to European monetary integration

Within the UK any debate about European monetary integration is at present overshadowed by the issue of whether or not sterling should join the ERM. It might be useful quickly to summarize some views on this. Basically the only serious opposition to this comes from the Prime Minister, though the monetary authorities would want to wait for relatively calm economic conditions before entering:

— both the TUC and the Labour Party have changed their views significantly on this issue (it was not long ago that the Labour Party supported UK withdrawal from the EC) – now both appear to support sterling participation in the ERM, no doubt influenced by the implacable opposition of the Prime Minister to this;

— the Confederation of British Industry supports entry, on the grounds that this would reduce both sterling's volatility and the likelihood of serious misalignments and would increase the possibility of lower UK interest rates, possibly by lowering the risk premium in sterling;

— the Foreign Office supports entry, partly on the economic grounds of the monetary authorities but also on wider political grounds, including the fear that the UK will lose much influence in Europe at a critical time by not joining:

— the Bank of England and the Treasury are in favour of entry in principle, partly on CBI grounds and partly because linking sterling to the Deutschmark would be the most obvious way of restoring confidence to UK monetary policy – nevertheless the governor of the Bank of England has expressed doubts about joining while the trade deficit and inflation pose pressing problems:

— Nigel Lawson rejected entry at the time of the 1983 review of the issue but has since supported entry – indeed he proposed a wider scheme of exchange rate stabilization involving all the major currencies; his successor, John Major, also appears to favour entry, though possibly with less conviction.

— the Prime Minister remains opposed (though sheltering behind the doctrine of unripe time) on the grounds that absolute primacy must be given to domestic monetary policy; doubts over the wisdom of intervening in the foreign exchange markets also play a part – current UK inflation problems are attributed by her to the decision to peg sterling to the DM during 1987/early 1988; during the 1989 Madrid Summit of the EC she conceded that sterling could eventually join the ERM but tied the decision to conditions that allow considerable latitude.

The wider issue of European monetary integration has so far been less controversial in the UK, perhaps because few have focused on the possible implications. Once again Mrs Thatcher is at one extreme on this, essentially being very sceptical of any significant change from the status quo. Indeed she was very much opposed to the Delors Report and only agreed to the first stage with great reluctance. However, Mrs Thatcher is much less isolated on the EMU issue than on sterling participation in the ERM. Most official opinion in the UK is hostile to any artificial or utopian moves to monetary union. The emphasis is very much more on a cautious and evolutionary approach, with moves to monetary union following in the wake of economic and financial integration. In particular the need to make significant progress on completing the single market programme and eliminating exchange controls elsewhere in the EC before embarking on further steps to monetary union has been stressed. Consistent with this John Major has proposed a scheme whereby the choice of a single currency would be determined by market forces and not by administrative fiat – towards this end he has proposed that individuals and businesses in the EC should be free to trade in and hold all community currencies.

7   Conclusions

During the 1980s British macroeconomic policy has in principle been markedly different from the Keynesian policies pursued during the postwar period, when the main objective was to fine-tune aggregate demand so as to achieve satisfactory levels of growth and employment. The essence of the new approach was set out in the Medium Term Financial Strategy; the primary aim became the control of inflation through the achievement of monetary targets aided by a tight fiscal policy. Interest rates were to be adjusted to whatever level necessary to achieve the monetary targets, with the exchange rate also free.

In practice fiscal policy has generally been tight. The

authorities achieved great success in bringing down inflation in the early 1980s but since then appear to have given priority to boosting growth. The clearly laid out monetary strategy of the MTFS has been abandoned following the collapse of the monetary targets. Considerable confusion exists about UK monetary policy but the authorities are currently trying to bring inflation under control by a policy of high interest rates (and a high exchange rate). Indeed the level of sterling is now an important consideration in UK monetary policy, though the exact target is rarely made clear.

The UK has played an active role in recent attempts at international macroeconomic policy coordination (the Plaza-Louvre process) though sterling remains outside the ERM. However, movements in the Deutschmark have had an increasing influence on exchange rate policy, reflecting the growing importance of the EC to UK trade. The weight of the Deutschmark in the sterling effective exchange rate index is now as large as that of the US dollar. The perceived need to preserve monetary independence currently prevents sterling participation in the ERM but the need to achieve a coherent base for monetary policy, allied with the impact of the 1992 process in further increasing the importance of EC currencies, suggests that sterling will eventually enter the ERM. Most informed opinion within the UK is in favour of this step, in part for political reasons, though some feel that the decision should be delayed until present excess demand pressures have abated. The Prime Minister has finally agreed in principle to sterling entry subject to certain conditions, including lower UK inflation and the abandonment of exchange controls in France and Italy.

5 The position of the Netherlands: A lesson in monetary union

Jan Q. Th. Rood

Introduction

As a result of the decision to complete the internal market within the EC by 1992, the issues of monetary integration, the creation of a European Central Bank (ECB) and a European currency are again at the top of the political agenda. According to many observers, further European monetary integration is a prerequisite to the full enjoyment of the benefits of the internal market programme, as computed in the well-known Cecchini Report. Monetary integration is all the more necessary since the decision of the European finance ministers to liberalize the flows of capital within the EC area, starting in July 1990. Such a liberalization could easily lead to an increased volatility of exchange rates within the present EMS framework.

Intensification of monetary integration in Europe may take different forms, ranging from strengthening the exchange rate mechanism (ERM) within the EMS to the outright creation of a fully-fledged economic and monetary union, i.e. including an ECB and European currency. It goes without saying that the Netherlands with its relatively small and open economy has a special interest in the form, modalities and process of further monetary integration. Leaving aside the political symbolism of the creation of Economic and Monetary Union as such, economic self-interest has historically been the driving force behind the pursuit by successive Dutch governments of trade liberalization and monetary stability (in Europe). Still, it must be stressed that not every step in the process of European unification necessarily reflects Dutch interests.

In section 1 of this chapter, the Dutch interest in economic openness and monetary stability will be discussed from the historical point of view. In section 2 we shall go into the present state of integration of the Dutch economy in the EC economy, the German economy in particular, and shall consider the implications of this state of affairs for monetary policy, particularly the extent of monetary autonomy of the Netherlands. In section 3 the main actor in the formation of this policy, the Dutch Central Bank, will be dealt with: its formal status, powers and instruments, and its relationship with the Treasury Department. From both these sections a number of conclusions will follow concerning the conditions set by Dutch authorities to further monetary integration within the EC. These conditions will be elaborated in section 5. The final section highlights the leading theme of this chapter: the Dutch interest in monetary stability with its main trading partners. This interest will be discussed in view of the Delors Report on monetary integration, as tabled during the EC Summit in Madrid (June 1989).

From the perspective laid down in the Delors Report, there is an additional reason to scrutinize further the Dutch position in the process of monetary integration in Europe. As will be made clear in section 2, through its 'special relationship' with West Germany (FRG) the exchange rate between the guilder and the Deutschmark is very close to being a fixed one. The room to pursue an independent monetary policy is very limited indeed, and may even be non-existent. This implies that maintenance of the external balance and of international competitiveness is increasingly influenced by domestic factors such as wage development, productivity growth and the control of government expenditure. This state of affairs places the Netherlands from a *substantive* (i.e. non-formal) point of view somewhere in the second stage of monetary integration as envisaged in the Delors Report. It clearly shows to other countries what can be expected from the implementation of the Delors proposals.

On the other hand, the Dutch position is the result of a highly asymmetrical relationship with the FRG; a situation which is hardly acceptable to the bigger EC members and which largely explains the present pursuit of more symmetrical monetary integration through the EMU.

1   The aims of Dutch foreign economic policy: continuity in a changing world

The integration of the Netherlands in the international and European economy is a historical fact that can easily be explained by its geographical location. As a coastal state situated on the delta of the Rhine, the Netherlands is bound to have a maritime tradition. It became the main transit area to the European hinterland, specifically to Germany and, after 1945, to the FRG. Its limited size and lack of natural resources have emphasized external dependence and are the basis of a strong commercial tradition. This imperative of commerce has been most eloquently formulated by the seventeenth-century Dutch statesman Johan de Witt: 'The interest of this state lies in this: that there be peace and quiet everywhere and that commerce be carried on unimpeded.'

Dutch foreign policy has consistently aimed at preserving 'peace and quiet' on the European continent. During the seventeenth century the balance of power was preserved, with England in the role as 'holder of the balance', and afterwards peace was enjoyed until 1940 through a policy of neutrality and aloofness. (See in particular Voorhoeve, 1979). After 1945 Dutch foreign policy and foreign economic policy developed within the framework of the Pax Americana created under the aegis of US economic and political hegemony.

The aims and methods of foreign *economic* policy throughout the centuries may be summarized under the following headings:

— *Economic openness*. In accordance with its geographical position and commercial tradition the Netherlands has consistently been an advocate of the principle of free trade. In this regard there seems to be no difference between the doctrine of 'freedom of the high seas' formulated by the seventeenth-century Dutch jurist Hugo Grotius in order to break the Portuguese colonial monopoly and the present government's position regarding Europe 1992 and beyond.[1]
— *Globalism of economic activities*. A global spread of economic activities (for example through direct investment) is meant to reduce the risks to a country as vulnerable as the Netherlands, specifically with regard to the import of commodities.[2]
— *Monetary stability*. Monetary stability has always been

considered crucial to the flourishing of international trade and investment and to the upholding of an open international economy. The creation of a system of rules imposing domestic monetary discipline, i.e. the obligation to maintain or restore the internal balance, is particularly crucial to a country as small and trade dependent as the Netherlands. The rules should especially bind those countries disposing of reserve currencies ('core countries') which by definition may have a destabilizing effect upon exchange rate stability. This consideration explains the Dutch preference for a system of *fixed* exchange rates. The imperative of monetary stability appeared *inter alia* between the wars when the Netherlands was among the last countries to leave the Gold Standard, perhaps to its own detriment.

— *Multilateralism*. The preference for a 'rule-governed' international monetary system is also a consequence of the position of the Netherlands. Too small to dictate the rules of the game and with too much to lose, it is in the Dutch interest to commit other states to a multilateral system of rules which guarantees monetary stability and economic openness. This also explains the emphasis on multilateralism as the preferred method of consultation and decision-making – multilateralism enables the building of coalitions and could prevent the formation of directorates of large countries[3] – and on the role of the IMF as objective monetary supervisor.

These considerations and interests elucidate the consistent striving by Dutch authorities for a system guaranteeing monetary discipline. In their view exchange rate stability starts at home and requires a prudent internal policy in the core countries; i.e. fixed exchange rates.

For these reasons, successive Dutch governments felt comfortable with the postwar Pax Americana and its formal reflection, the Bretton Woods system. In principle, this system guaranteed progressive liberalization of world trade through the reduction of tariffs and the maintenance of monetary stability through dollar–gold parity. Multilateralism was the main method of economic diplomacy. But Dutch foreign policy cannot be judged by developments in the first decade after the Second World War. The European economies were in a phase of recovery; Marshall aid was at this stage more important than economic openness and monetary stability. Moreover, the European currencies were not yet convertible. Internationally, the economy was in a process of *normalization* under American leadership.

1958 appears to be a crucial year. European currencies became convertible again. Economic integration in Europe reached a qualitatively new stage through the adoption of the Treaty of Rome, which founded the EC. The Western world was on the threshold of a real liberalization of international trade negotiated during the Dillon and Kennedy rounds (GATT). One might say that from 1958 onwards the conditions under which Bretton Woods could be put to trial were there.

And Bretton Woods was put to trial. The balance of payments deficit of the US became a problem as the need for liquidity in the rest of the world lessened. At the same time the reserve position of the US worsened dramatically. During the 1960s the so-called 'Triffin dilemma' – the potential contradiction between liquidity creation and reliability of the key currency as anchor of the system – became visible. From the Dutch point of view, this meant that while the need for monetary discipline became more pressing, the fundamentals of the post-war monetary regime started to erode rapidly as a result of the decline of US hegemony. The subsequent demise of the Bretton Woods system meant that the Dutch 'ideal' of an *international* monetary system could no longer be realized.

In response to the monetary turbulence of the 1960s and 1970s, orientation towards Europe/the EC as a framework for stability gradually grew in importance. In addition to the end of Bretton Woods, there are a number of other reasons for this shift:

— Since the loss of the colonies in Asia (the Indonesian archipelago) the economic importance, in terms of trade, of the European hinterland increased.
— Germany, the main Dutch trading partner, became more dominant within the EC.
— Despite 'Eurosclerosis', factual and formal economic integration within the EC proceeded during the 1970s, as a result of which Dutch policy autonomy decreased.
— It appeared possible to realize, within the framework of the European monetary arrangement, several objectives that are important from a Dutch point of view, which due to American opposition could not be realized at an international level.[4]

Although in view of the Dutch preference for a multilateral monetary system the European option is only second best, these factors explain why this option became more and more important. When the US was no longer able or willing to perform its role as 'stabilizer' and, instead, became itself a source of monetary instability, there was no other choice than to opt for Europe. For economic reasons (exchange rate stability, trade) as well as for political reasons (to strengthen the negotiating position *vis-à-vis* the US), the EC became the main route to openness and stability, although on a regional level.

2 Monetary policy today: the German imperative

Key concepts in Dutch monetary policy are 'balance' and 'stability'. The principal aim of monetary policy is to maintain the internal and external value of the currency. The connection between the two is the inflation rate. An increase of domestic inflation will lead to a deterioration of the external balance, increasing pressure on the exchange rate, and subsequently the import of inflation from abroad. In the end, economic growth and employment, no doubt, will be affected.

The need for a consistently low level of relative inflation is the more urgent for an economy as open and as internationalized as the Dutch is today. The extent of openness of the Dutch economy can be illustrated by the so-called export ratio, i.e. export of goods and services as a percentage of GNP. For the Netherlands, this amounts to 50 per cent. By comparison, for the US the export/GNP ratio is 10 per cent, for Japan 13 per cent, for France 20 per cent, for Germany 30 per cent, and for Belgium/Luxembourg 60 per cent. Domestic price stability – i.e. the rate of inflation related to the main trading partners – is a primary tool in maintaining the competitiveness of the export sector.

On the other hand, the Netherlands is highly dependent on imports, and as such is vulnerable to externalities. These concern not only inflation transferred through the exchange rates, but also exchange rate instability as such and changes in commodity prices, especially the oil price.[5]

Therefore, as was contended in section 1, the Dutch authorities have consistently advocated an international system of fixed exchange rates, which is thought to be a stimulus to international trade. Even more crucial, in view of the domestic policy of the US and the experiences of the 1970s, a system of fixed exchange rates will impose a certain discipline on the internal policy of *other* countries. The objective of Dutch monetary diplomacy, then, has been 'to promote the establishment of an international monetary system that would provide participating countries with the maximum incentives to restore *internal* equilibrium' (Szasz, 1988, p. 322).

At the international level, Dutch monetary diplomacy has not been very successful, though. For it is only since 1985 that the non-system of flexible exchange rates has been replaced by some form of exchange rate management. The Netherlands, however, has been excluded from its main decision-making body, the G7. In the mean time the Dutch authorities saw their distrust of floating rates confirmed in the form of mounting inflation, excessive exchange rate instability and rising protectionism.

Following the demise of the Bretton Woods system the Dutch monetary posture shifted to the European theatre. In 1972 the Netherlands joined the 'snake' and remained a member despite the withdrawal of the UK, Italy and France. The 'mini-snake' provided the Netherlands with the required monetary stability in economic relations with its two main trading partners, Germany and Belgium. This consideration was also fundamental to the decision to join the EMS.

Membership of the EMS is indeed rather obvious from the point of view of the geographical distribution of Dutch trade. As illustrated by Table 5.1, the EC is by far the most important trading area for the Netherlands.

Table 5.1. Imports and exports by countries of origin and destination (1987)

| | Shares (%) | |
	Imports	Exports
World	100	100
Europe	81	84
EC	64	75
FRG	27	27
USA	7	4
Japan	3	1

Source: Central Bureau voor de Statistiek (1988) *Statistical Handbook 1988*, The Hague, p. 232.

Through the EMS 63 per cent of Dutch exports and 54 per cent of its imports are controlled by a regime providing monetary stability.

What appears most clearly from Table 5.1, though, is the strong economic interrelationship between the Dutch and the German economy. The FRG is by far the most important trading partner of the Netherlands – Belgium and Luxembourg being in second place with a share of only 14 per cent in imports and exports. The Netherlands, in turn, is, next to France, Germany's second major trading partner, accounting for about 10 per cent of its imports and exports.[6] This illustrates the fact that the mutual relationship is highly asymmetrical.

Given its dependence on Germany, the deflationary anchor of the EMS, the Dutch authorities have very little room for an independent monetary policy. For deviation from German monetary policy may easily lead to higher inflation, loss of faith in the guilder, higher interest rates and a worsening of the external balance. For these reasons upholding the exchange rate between the guilder and the Deutschmark has absolute priority in Dutch monetary policy. Four *de facto* 'rules of the game' are implicit in this policy:

Although in the short term a depreciation of the guilder *vis-à-vis* the Deutschmark may favour exports to Germany, in the longer term this will lead to inflationary pressure because of rising import prices, and to an overall deterioration in the export position. Therefore the Dutch guilder should not depreciate in relation to the German mark. On the contrary, it should be as strong as possible within the EMS intervention margins, even when the Deutschmark is in a relatively weak position. In this way inflationary pressure is resisted. Furthermore, a strong position of the guilder is considered important in upholding faith in the currency, and enables the authorities to make *selective* use of the interest rate weapon in stabilizing exchange rates. In addition, international confidence in the guilder is considered important because of the need to finance the budget deficit and in order to stimulate economic growth through relatively low interest rates. The only criterion for the effectiveness of Dutch monetary policy, then, is the question to what extent the authorities have been able to maintain a fixed exchange rate between guilder and the Deutschmark. As can be seen in Figure 5.1, they have been rather successful in this.

The interest rate, i.e. the discount rate, is the main instrument in upholding monetary stability. The desirability of

Figure 5.1 Guilders per Deutschmark

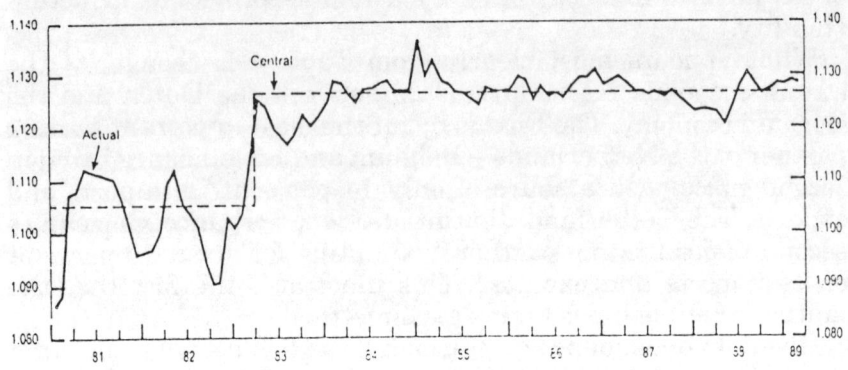

changes in this rate is considered primarily, and perhaps *only*, in view of the priority of exchange rate stability in the Dutch–German relationship. This means that other objectives of economic policy are subordinate to this and that the scope of monetary policy is rather limited.

This implies particularly that the Dutch discount rate should not be allowed to deviate substantially from the German discount rate. This would only lead to undesirable pressure on the guilder. So changes in the official German rates are, depending upon the position of guilder and Deutschmark within the EMS, usually followed by the Dutch authorities.

Finally, in the case of an official realignment within the EMS, the guilder is to devalue or, as usually happens, revalue along

Table 5.2. Realignment within the EMS

	Bel/ Lux franc	Danish Krone	French franc	Deutsch- mark	Irish punt	Italian lire	Dutch guilder
24. 9.79		−2.86		2.00			
30.11.79		−4.76					
23. 3.81						−6.00	
5.10.81			−3.00	5.50		−3.00	5.50
22. 2.82	−8.50	−3.00					
14. 6.82			−5.75	4.25		−2.75	4.25
21. 3.83	1.50	2.50	−2.50	5.50	−3.50	−2.50	3.50
22. 7.85						−7.84	
7. 4.86	1.00	1.00	−3.00	3.00			3.00
5. 8.86					−8.00		
12. 1.87	2.00			3.00			3.00

with the German mark. As shown in Table 5.2, only in two cases (September 1979 and March 1983) was the revaluation of the guilder smaller than the Deutschmark's revaluation.

The conclusion of a number of authors is that in view of the asymmetry in the German–Dutch relationship, the authorities have no choice other than to follow the German lead (see, *inter alia*, De Grauwe, 1989). The sanction on deviation is severe: a loss of international confidence in the guilder, higher interest rates and inflation and consequently lower economic growth. In this respect, one may wonder whether the Netherlands has any monetary independence at all.

The same authors conclude that from the perspective of the EMS system as a whole, there really are two regimes within this area: the German–Dutch regime (the non-EMS members Austria and Switzerland also belong to this regime) based on a highly asymmetrical relationship and very limited monetary autonomy of the junior partner(s), and a regime consisting of Germany and the other EMS members (see De Grauwe, 1989;

Figure 5.2 Budget deficits (% of GNP)

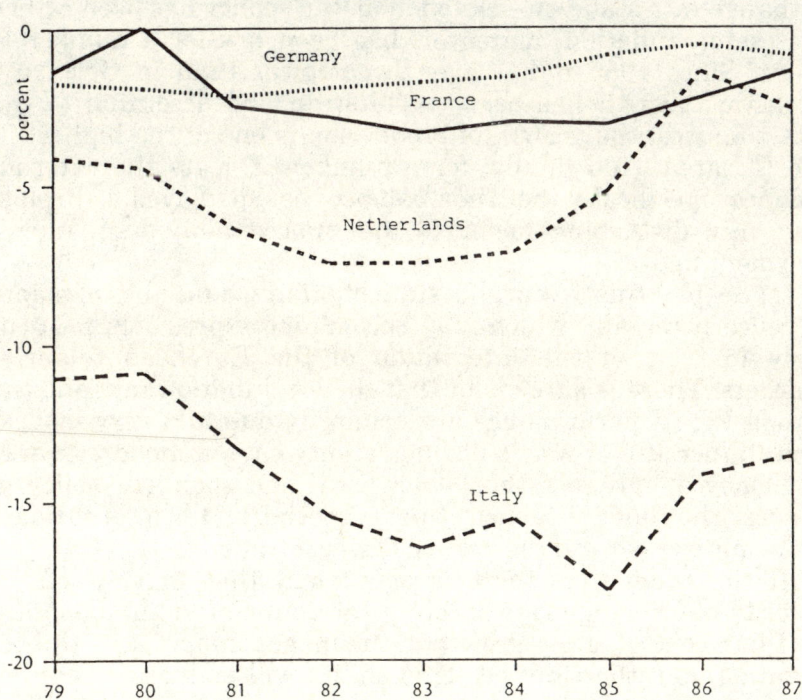

Fase and Huijser, 1988). The existence of two regimes is confirmed by figures on growth of the money supply, the course of inflation and the interest rates. In all respects the Dutch position is much closer to the German position than in the case of, for example, France and Italy (see De Grauwe, 1989).

Loss of monetary independence does not imply, though, that the Netherlands is completely stripped of economic autonomy. Contrary to what the Delors Report suggests with regard to budget deficits, in the Dutch case a relatively large budget deficit has been compatible with the maintenance of monetary stability *vis-à-vis* the Deutschmark. As illustrated in Figure 5.2, the Dutch budgetary stance differs considerably from the German position.

What counts primarily regarding the relationship between budget deficit and external stability is the way in which the deficit is financed. As long as the deficit is financed through the capital market, specifically the domestic market – as in the Netherlands – no negative impact upon the external position can be traced at all.

One may conclude that with regard to its principle aim – exchange rate stability – Dutch monetary policy has been rather successful. Inflation, moreover, has been low for a number of years. Since 1985 it has even been lower than in Germany. Economic growth has been catching up and according to the latest figures, the growth of production is one of the highest in the EC area. And finally, for a number of years the external balance, specifically the trade balance, has displayed a surplus. The only disturbing factor is the unacceptably high unemployment figure.

Yet despite this favourable state of affairs, a number of points of concern remain, which may become more pressing, particularly in view of the integration of the European financial markets. There is agreement that the low inflation rate and the strong export performance are primarily due to a very modest overall increase of wages during recent years, a modest growth in money supply, a rather strict fiscal and spending policy to reduce the budget deficit and, especially, to international economic growth and the growth of world trade.

At the same time there is agreement that in view of the priority of exchange rate stability the contribution of monetary policy to control of the growth of the money supply, and thus of inflation, is rather limited. This ability will be further reduced as integration of the European money markets proceeds. As a result, the emphasis in the control of liquidity creation will shift even more to domestic factors, such as moderation of wages and a restrictive budget policy, not only to counter inflation but also to maintain and improve the export position of Dutch industry and commerce.

But in this respect tensions do emerge. First, after years of moderation, pressures for a substantial rise in wages are increasing, in both the private and public sectors. Second, as appears from Table 5.3, the Dutch budget deficit is by comparison still large.

Table 5.3. Budget balances in a number of countries (% of GNP)

	1987	1988
United States	−2.3	−1.8
Japan	−0.3	−0.1
Germany	−1.8	−2.0
France	−2.5	−1.6
United Kingdom	−1.5	+0.2
Italy	−10.5	−10.6
Netherlands	−6.2	−4.9
Belgium	−7.2	−7.1

The same conclusion applies to the official debt, which is one of the largest within the OECD area. Only Ireland, Belgium and Italy have a larger debt. The official debt, moreover, grew rapidly from 46 per cent in 1980 to 74 per cent of GNP in 1986, and is estimated to rise to 90 per cent of GNP in 1990. The interest payments as a percentage of national income and government budget have also increased rapidly. In 1990 they will amount to 13 per cent of the budget. Because of the debt and budget deficit the risk of monetary financing, and thus of an increase in the money supply, still looms in the background.

This is disturbing in view of the actual development of liquidity creation. As shown in Table 5.4, the growth of the money supply accelerated during 1988 and is clearly above the implicit target of 5 per cent informally agreed upon between the Central Bank and commercial banks.[7]

The rapid expansion of the money supply during the first quarter of 1989 necessitated a formal agreement between Central Bank and commercial banks to limit liquidity creation during the period April 1989–June 1990 to a growth of 6.25 per cent.[8] At the same time a new monetary instrument, the

Table 5.4. Growth of money supply (M2)

	1979–81	1982–85	1986	1987	1988
Liquidity creation from abroad	−1.4	4.2	−5.6	1.9	4.6
Domestic liquidity creation	7.1	4.9	8.8	2.9	9.8
Increase in money supply	5.7	9.1	3.2	4.8	14.4

Source: Dutch Central Bank (1988) *Annual Report 1988*, Amsterdam, p. 67.

so-called cash reserve requirement, was introduced to implement this goal.

An analysis of Dutch monetary policy shows that the extent of the Netherlands' monetary autonomy is rather limited. The asymmetrical relation with Germany means that there is hardly any room for an independent interest and money supply policy. On the contrary, upholding the exchange rate between guilder and Deutschmark has priority. In the mean time domestic factors have become more important in the struggle against inflation. In view of recent developments in the domestic field it may be expected that the tension between external and internal stability will increase.

3   The main actor: the Central Bank

The Dutch Central Bank – *De Nederlandse Bank* – which is located in Amsterdam, was founded in 1814 on the initiative of King William I. During the nineteenth century its main task was to act as a *private* bank and to supply credit to the commercial and industrial sectors of the economy. Only as a secondary function did the Bank issue banknotes.[9] In due course, however, the Bank started to perform the functions which characterize a modern central bank, i.e. to act as a banker's bank. The main reason for this evolution was the development of commercial banks, which borrowed from the Central Bank; a development which provides the latter with the interest rate as a monetary weapon. After the Second World

War, the supply of credit to the private sector was left to the commercial banks. From then onwards the Central Bank has acted as a central bank in the proper sense. In 1948 the Bank was nationalized, with the state as its only shareholder.

Despite state ownership, the Central Bank is to a large extent autonomous in exercising its policy. This independence is based on and guaranteed by the Bank Law of 1948. The organizational structure of the Bank, specifically the way the directors are appointed and their term of office, the payment and pension schemes of Bank officials, the definition of its functions, and the dispute settlements procedure between Bank and government, i.e. the finance minister, show its independence.

The organizational structure of the Bank consists of a Directorate, a Board of Commissioners and a Bank Council. The Directorate is the policy-making body. It consists of a president (presently Dr W. Duisenberg), a director-secretary and four directors. They are appointed by the government for a tenure of seven years, which is longer than any government can hope to be in office. The members of the directorate can be reappointed. The Board of Commissioners (twelve members) is a supervising body; its main task is to approve of the yearly account. The government is represented on this board by a 'royal commissioner', who is also president of the Bank Council (of seventeen). This is an advisory body to both the Bank and the government. The Council consists of, *inter alia*, representatives of labour unions and the business community, and of monetary experts.

The main functions of the Central Bank are defined in the Bank Law of 1948. They concern:

— the issue of notes and coins;
— the function of cashier of the state;
— the management of the official reserves;
— supervision of the private banking sector.

The *main* task though, as formulated in the Bank Law, is to safeguard the value of the currency in such a way that the economy will benefit from it. This means that the Bank's primary function is to maintain price stability; i.e. the domestic and external purchasing power of the guilder. In order to achieve this, the Bank regulates the money supply and intervenes in the exchange markets. Realignment of the exchange rate, however, is the province of the finance minister.

Regarding the maintenance of price stability, the Bank is only responsible for monetary and credit policy. Price stability, though, depends heavily upon overall economic policy, including budget and fiscal policy, social policy (incomes, social security and wages), and so on. This division of labour may lead to conflicts of interest between the Central Bank and the finance minister in particular, who is *politically* responsible for budget and fiscal policy. Conflicts are usually prevented by intensive consultation among both the Bank's president and the minister. But if a conflict should emerge, the Bank Law provides for a dispute settlement procedure. In such a case, the finance minister is empowered to order the Central Bank to change its policy in accordance with the government's goals. But the Bank is subsequently entitled to appeal against this directive, to the 'crown' (an administrative litigation procedure). The government, in turn, is accountable to parliament for its decision. Up until now no need has arisen to use this procedure. It emphasizes, however, on the one hand the ultimate political responsibility of the elected authorities. On the other hand, because of its political weight, it stresses the bank's policy leeway and autonomy.

In order to safeguard external and internal stability, the Central Bank uses a number of instruments. These instruments can be distinguished with regard to the two principal aims of monetary policy: maintenance of external exchange rate stability and management of domestic money supply.

Stability of exchange rates is pursued through intervention in the money market (direct or on term) or through changes in short-term interest rates. Within the second category, changes in the discount rate, changes in rates of open-market transactions (the most often used) and the introduction of reserve requirements can be identified.

Growth of domestic money supply stems from three sources: granting of bank credit to the private sector, monetary financing by government, and a surplus on the balance of payments. The Bank's instruments to regulate the money supply are only directed to the first of these sources. In principle it has two types of instrument at its disposal: direct and indirect. The first involves the setting of quantitative limits or ceilings to the access of commercial banks to credit. The second functions through the price mechanism, i.e. the interest rate, in order to change the amount of liquidity. As the interest rate is primarily used as a means to stabilize exchange rates, emphasis in the regulation of the money supply has tended to fall upon the setting of restrictions. The effectiveness of this instrument has declined, however, as a result of the integration of financial markets. For this reason the Central Bank has recently introduced two new instruments to manage the growth of money supply: the use of open-market operations in government bonds and the introduction of the so-called cash-reserve requirement for private banks. These instruments were introduced mainly because of the fast growth of the money supply in 1988, as illustrated in section 2.

4   Monetary integration through gradualism

In view of the Dutch interest in a system of fixed exchange rates (see section 1) and the experiences with the European exchange rate mechanism, it should not cause any surprise that successive Dutch governments and the Central Bank have always been supporters of further monetary integration with Europe and the creation of an EMU. As was stated in a white paper on monetary integration: 'The final goal of monetary integration within the EC is the creation of an Economic and Monetary Union.'[10] But not every step in this process is acceptable. On the contrary, on the basis of the preceding sections a clear set of conclusions can be drawn about the requirements for further monetary integration and the preferred route to an EMU.

With regard to the three routes which in principle are available to the creation of an EMU – monetary integration through the ECU, the institutional 'big bang' and the gradual approach towards integration through monetary and economic convergence – the Dutch Central Bank and successive Dutch governments are clearly in favour of the third option. In the well-known debate between 'monetarists' and 'economists', they are firmly embedded in the second camp. Or as Dr Szasz – a director of the Central Bank – remarks with regard to the difference between the Dutch and the 'monetarist' view of monetary integration: 'whereas the "monetarists" meant credit the Dutch meant discipline' (1988, p. 327; also see Szasz, 1989).

Further convergence of economic and monetary policy among the EC member states is, in the view of the Dutch government and the Central Bank, a prerequisite to such institutional steps as the creation of a European Central Bank (ECB) or the issue of a European currency. In a recent government paper about

European integration, convergence of economic and monetary policy was even called a *'conditio sine qua non'* to further monetary integration.[11]

For this reason, the route to integration through the ECU – favoured among others by Dutch industrialists[12] – is not supported. Although authorities have not been unfavourable to a wider private use of the ECU, there are strong reservations about its use as a parallel currency. The issuing of such a currency presupposes the existence of an institution responsible for its creation, i.e. an ECB (in embryo). An ECB only makes sense, though, if there is more convergence among the EC economies. And the creation of a thirteenth currency may have an inflationary effect, as its creation and subsequent impact upon national money supplies cannot be controlled domestically. Finally, precisely for countries with a strong currency, the ECU, being a basket currency, is not attractive because of its relative weakness. Indeed, from this point of view the recent entry of the peseta and escudo into the ECU currency basket may be considered a 'deterioration in quality'.[13]

The conditions for monetary integration through institutional reform as called for by, *inter alia*, France and Italy, are also lacking according to this view. Although inflation rates have narrowed, important differences remain. The same applies to the size of the budget deficits and of the official debt of the EC member states. These differences will not be corrected through institutional reform. On the contrary, a certain distrust can be observed with regard to the real intentions of the European 'monetarists'. In view of the French dissatisfaction with the monetary hegemony of Germany, the wish of France, Italy and Spain to have institutional reform is considered a means to loosen the deflationary grip of the Bundesbank, which is not acceptable to the Dutch monetary authorities. Indeed, in the words of the director of the Central Bank quoted above, the Dutch prefer discipline to credit. Moreover, in view of the fact that Portugal is still not a member of the EMS, that Spain has only recently joined the mechanism, that the UK and Greece do not participate in the ERM, that Belgium has two exchange rates, that Italy and Spain have a wider fluctuation margin, and that capital has only been fully liberalized in Germany, Denmark, the UK and the Netherlands, it appears to be rather premature to consider a quantum leap such as the founding of an ECB.

Nor is institutional reform and the creation of a system of fixed exchange rates in an early stage of European monetary integration acceptable to the monetary philosophy of the Dutch authorities. The key concept in monetary stability is *reliability*. Stability of exchange rates will only be attained if the market expects the authorities to stick to the rates and/or margins agreed upon. If this commitment cannot be sustained, speculation will follow. Realignment of exchange rates will become inevitable. Reliability will only emerge if the rates agreed upon are realistic in view of the economic fundamentals and if the authorities are prepared to give priority to upholding them, as is the case in the Dutch–German relation (cf. section 2). Under such circumstances it will also become possible to reduce differences in interest rates (on the problem of reliability, see De Grauwe, 1989, p. 14).

Within the EMS as a whole, priorities and economic fundamentals differ. The system has, in the Dutch view, only been successful because of its *flexibility*, i.e. relatively wide but therefore sustainable fluctuation margins for the weaker-currency countries. This flexibility has discouraged speculation and resulted in an exchange rate practice which resembles the so-called 'crawling peg': adjustment of exchange rates through small steps without causing speculative crises. The logical implication of this view is that further monetary integration can only take place through convergence of national economic and monetary policies. The need for such a cautious approach has increased since the decision to liberalize capital within the EC area, as this measure may lead to more speculation in order to test the reliability of the present exchange rates.

The only route to monetary integration considered realistic, then, is the gradual approach of economic convergence and of strengthening present monetary cooperation within the EMS framework. From this premiss, a process of monetary integration consisting of three stages can be defined:

1. A material stage;
2. an institutional stage;
3. a 'crowning' stage (*Krönungs-Phase*).

Stage 1

This stage consists of three interrelated steps: (1) free movement of capital within the EC area in accordance with the 1992 programme; (2) more convergence of national economic and monetary policies in accordance with the convergence directive of 1974; and (3) strengthening of the EMS.

The free movement of capital within the EC was agreed by the finance ministers in June 1988. It is considered important not only for its favourable effect on the supply side of the European economy, but also because free capital may stimulate a further convergence of monetary policies. The only point of concern to the Netherlands, apart from the actual implementation of the directive by 1992, is the increasing risk of tax evasion.

During this first stage, the *conditio sine qua non* to EMU should be realized, i.e. the further convergence of monetary and economic policy and performance among the member states. A low level of inflation in all member states is considered a prerequisite of more stable exchange rates. In this stage too, the size of the budget deficits should be discussed. The argument for this is twofold. First, a large budget deficit may require monetary financing and increase inflationary pressure within the EC area. Second, a large budget deficit may lead to a disproportionally large demand for capital on the money market and a subsequent upward pressure on European interest rates. These arguments underline the need for an *independent* ECB, to be created in stages 2/3.

In stage 1 convergence will primarily take place, though, through a strengthening and more intensive use of the existing EC procedures – the Council of Finance Ministers, the Committee of Governors of Central Banks, the Monetary Committee, etc. – on the basis of the convergence decision of 1974. More intensive use of these procedures, multilateral surveillance by means of economic indicators and exchange of information may stimulate economic and monetary convergence. But in this stage decisions will be non-binding.

Next, convergence of policy and performance will also be stimulated by strengthening the EMS. In particular those countries which are not members of the EMS/ERM and which have to cope with high inflation may benefit from participation. Participation of all EC countries in the EMS/ERM is a condition, then, of the next stages. They should eventually participate, though, on equal terms, i.e. within a fluctuation margin of 2.25 per cent.[14]

The transition from stage 1 to the next stages consists of a further narrowing of the fluctuation margins. Only if the present EMS/ERM is able to cope with the entry of high-inflation countries and the free movement of capital (reliability) will it be possible to start the institutional stages, which actually implies that this phase can only start after the establishment of fixed exchange rates.

Stages 2 and 3

Whereas stage 1 is developed outside the legal framework of the EC treaty, in stage 2, economic and monetary cooperation need to be incorporated within this framework. According to the Dutch Central Bank and government, this is a logical step, as during stages 2 and 3 monetary and budgetary policy will be more and more centralized within the Community, eventually on the basis of *binding* decisions. This means that sovereignty will be formally transferred from the national to the Community level; a step which can only take place through a treaty revision. In this stage the relationship among, on the one hand, the Community institutions – Commission, Parliament, Council and the newly created ECB – should be determined, next to, on the other hand, the relationship between the Community and its member states – on the basis of the principle of 'subsidiarity'.[15] This demands a treaty revision through which the formal requirements of further monetary integration – the status of the Central Bank, its functions, etc. – will be arranged. Preparations for a treaty revision will, of course, take place during stage 1 through an intergovernmental conference (see Article 236 of the EC treaty).

The introduction of a common currency would be considered only after the institutional stage has been successfully completed. Such a step is explicitly presented as the *tailpiece* of monetary integration.

A fully-fledged EMU must meet the following conditions:

1. The issue of a common currency ought to be the sole responsibility of a European Central Bank, federally or unitarily organized;
2. The ECB needs to be independent from political authorities, comparable to the present position of the German and Dutch central banks. This means primarily that the ECB cannot be obliged to finance budget deficits. Moreover, the ECB would be the only responsible authority for the money supply, the interest rates and intervention with regard to external exchange rate stability,
3. The *primary* task of the ECB is to maintain the purchasing power of the common currency; i.e. the maintenance of price stability is its main function. External exchange rate stability should only be pursued in accordance with this task.

4. Parallel to monetary integration, the budget and fiscal policy of member states should be centralized with regard to the size and financing of budget deficits.
5. In accordance with the rule 'no taxation without representation', centralization of budget and fiscal policy requires a strengthening of parliamentary control by the European Parliament.

Not surprisingly the implementation of these conditions will result in the creation of a German/Dutch type of ECB/EMU, primarily characterized by a separation of monetary and political responsibilities. Apart from a tradition of monetary discipline and independence, this 'ideal type' has mainly been inspired by the fear that countries which are more prone to inflation would have too great an influence and the conviction that Dutch economic interests are best served by monetary stability.

5   Conclusion

Unlike the United Kingdom, the Netherlands until now has not witnessed a controversy about European monetary integration. The publication of the Delors Report has not given rise to heated debates about the loss of sovereignty or political fights between government and opposition. On the contrary, among the main political parties, and in parliament and the government there is consensus on the need for further monetary integration and eventually a fully-fledged EMU. The creation of such a union is considered to be the next logical step in the process of integration, i.e. after the completion of the internal market. During a debate in the parliamentary commission on European affairs on the occasion of the Madrid Summit, the Delors Report was thought to be a good starting point for further monetary integration. The only criticism concerned the need to harmonize budget policy and the need for a more intensive European structural policy in order to strengthen the EC's social cohesion.

The approval of the Delors Report should not come as a surprise. The three stages as set out in the report resemble more or less the stages mentioned in section 4. The Delors committee has clearly adopted an 'economist' approach as the starting point of monetary integration, which appears specifically from the measures to be taken during the first stage defined in the report. Moreover, it underlines the independence of the ECB and the goal of price stability.

Apart from its agreement with the Dutch view of monetary integration, the lack of opposition may, indeed, be explained by the fact that most continental EC member states are already used to a strong counter-inflationary policy (see Norman, 1989). This applies, as was seen in section 4, particularly to the Netherlands. Through its special relationship with Germany, Dutch monetary policy already exhibits all the features which are the goal of the first stage of the Delors Report. In this respect, implementation of this stage does not seem to have great implications for the Netherlands.

But Dutch support for the second and third stages of the Delors Report should not be taken for granted. First, because exchange rate stability with its main trading partners is vital to the Dutch economy, one may expect the Netherlands to stress the implementation of the economic and monetary conditions of stage 1 *on a Community-wide level*, before starting the next stages. And it is not very likely that Dutch officials will press too hard for monetary integration beyond stage 1, as long as there is no reliable alternative to the German anchor. In this respect, there is an explicit coalition between Germany and the Netherlands. For this reason as well, one may expect Dutch officials not to be too unhappy with British opposition to monetary union.

Second, although according to the Delors Report the ECB should be independent and with price stability as its main task, the actual implementation of these conditions will take place during the intergovernmental conference and by treaty revision. In view of the French and Italian positions with regard to a central bank, the outcome of these negotiations is unpredictable but decisive for Dutch agreement to the creation of a central bank.

On the other hand, in the well-known debate over priority between stability and employment, there has recently been some criticism, among others by the finance minister, of the Central Bank's decision to follow the 1 per cent interest rate increase unilaterally decided by the Bundesbank (6 October 1989). According to Central Bank authorities, this step had to be followed because of the priority of exchange rate stability with the Deutschmark (see section 2). This measure was, however, most unwelcome in view of the persistently high unemployment figures, which according to some require a more expansionary budget policy by government and low interest rates (see, *inter alia*, Ploeg, 1989). This refers to a longstanding debate about whether a country as open as the Netherlands has any room at all to pursue an independent economic policy, particularly to stimulate economic growth. This problem may gain importance in view of the recent change of government (fall 1989) from centre-right to centre-left. But as the real margin of economic autonomy is very small, it may be strongly doubted whether this debate will lead to a change of position on monetary integration. It is reasonably fair to assume that in this respect too, *continuity* will prevail as the main feature of the Dutch stance on monetary integration.

Notes

1. According to computations of the Dutch Central Planning Bureau (Centraal Plan Bureau), the Netherlands will profit relatively more than other EC member states from the implementation of the 1992 programme as it already has an open and trade-oriented economy.
2. A feature which appeared painfully during the oil crisis of 1973, but which is a permanent risk to an economy as open as the Dutch one.
3. This also explains Dutch opposition to the G7. The locus of monetary decision-making should be the IMF, particularly the Group of Ten and the Interim Committee. In reaction to the increased activity of the G7 since the Plaza agreement of 1985, the Netherlands has suggested a combined G7 membership of the Benelux countries. This has been refused, though, as the EC Commission is considered to take care of the interests of the smaller EC member states.
4. For an analysis of the shift of monetary policy from the international to the European level, see Szasz (1988).
5. This vulnerability appeared when, as a result of a drop in the oil prices, the revenues from the export of natural gas decreased dramatically; a development which caused serious budgetary problems for the Dutch government.
6. Recently there has been some deterioration in the Dutch trading position *vis-à-vis* the FRG as a result of, *inter alia*, a shift in the locus of economic activities within the Federal Republic. See Koopman and Paridon (1989, pp. 643–8).
7. Unlike other countries, no official monetary target is published by the Central Bank.
8. Stabilization of the money supply takes place only through control of the domestic sources of liquidity creation, which means the commercial banks. Liquidity supply from abroad and by government cannot be controlled by the Central Bank. The

acceptable increase is defined on the basis of (1) the long-term expected growth of production (3%); (2) the expected inflation (1%); and (3) the fact that the commercial sector is only responsible for 75% of the liquidity creation. On the basis of this calculation a yearly growth of 5% is considered acceptable.

9. Since 1849 the Netherlands has a uniform monetary system, i.e. with centrally issued banknotes and coins.
10. Tweede Kamer (Parliament) *The Long-term Goals of the EMS and ECU*, TK 1985–6, 19154, nr. 1–2, pp. 3–4 (in Dutch).
11. Tweede Kamer (Parliament) *Building to Europe*, TK 1988–9, 20596, nr. 6 (in Dutch).
12. In particular the Dutch electronics company Philips has been an advocate of the parallel use of the ECU. Through its presidency of the Round Table of European Industries, Philips has been able to lobby for this idea.
13. *International Herald Tribune*, 19 July 1989. See also Duisenberg (1989, pp. 185–90).
14. See SER (1986).
15. This principle was emphasized during the EC summit in Madrid (June 1989).

References

De Grauwe, P. (1989) *The European Monetary System and the Autonomy of Economic Policy*, The Hague (in Dutch).

Duisenberg, W.F. (1989) 'The ECU as a parallel currency', pp. 185–90 in *Report on Economic and Monetary Union in the European Community*, Luxembourg (paper submitted by the Dutch Central Bank director to the Delors Committee).

Fase, A.G.M. and A.P. Huijser (1988) 'Financial internationalization and worldwide integration of stock exchanges', (*Economisch-Statistische Berichten*), 30 March: 326-31 (in Dutch).

Koopman, G.J. and C.W.A.M. Paridon (1989) 'The economic relations between the Netherlands and Germany', *ESB*, 5 July: 643–8 (in Dutch).

Norman, Peter (1989) 'Sovereignty and fiscal policy', *The Financial Times*, 18 July.

Ploeg, F. van der (1989) *Towards Monetary Integration in Europe*, The Hague.

SER [Social and Economic Council] (1986) *Advisory Opinion on Economic and Monetary Cooperation within the EC*, The Hague (in Dutch).

Szasz, A. (1988) *Monetary Diplomacy: Dutch International Monetary Policy 1958–1987*, Leiden/Antwerp (in Dutch).

Szasz, A. (1989) *The Political Economy of the European Currency*, Rotterdam (in Dutch).

Voorhoeve, J.J.C. (1979) *Peace, Profits and Principles: a Study of Dutch Foreign Policy*, The Hague.

6 Conclusions and prospects for EMU

The creation of a monetary union involves the establishment of a single monetary authority and the conduct of a single monetary policy. In Chapter 1 we reviewed some of the factors influencing the costs and benefits that such a union may entail. Chapters 2 to 5 set out the political and economic features of monetary policy-making in the four countries of our study. The naure of cross-national similarities and differences will help determine the costs and benefits of an EMU across this representative sub-group of the EMS. In this chapter we compare and summarize the essential areas of convergence and conflict on the way to EMU. These relate to the economic objectives of monetary policy, its implementation (institutional and technical) and, finally, the political objectives and attitudes towards EMU that shape the debate within each country. We conclude with an assessment of the prospects for monetary union in the 1990s.

Economic objectives of monetary policy

During the last two decades both the theory and the practice of monetary policy have undergone profound change. The theoretical debate has revolved around the respective roles of fiscal and monetary policy in controlling inflation and promoting growth. The practice has seen a shift towards more market-oriented tools – interest rate changes and government bond sales/purchases – and away from direct controls on credit or interest rates in the domestic market. The direction of change has been similar across the four countries studied but the pace and pattern have varied.

Germany has probably seen the least change in its monetary policy objectives. As an outgrowth of its experience of

148

hyperinflation after the world wars, the Deutsche Bundesbank Act of 1957 charged the new central bank 'to regulate the amount of currency and credit in circulation ... with the aim of safeguarding the currency'. In the past twenty years the Bundesbank has interpreted its mandate to specify price stability as the primary objective of monetary policy, and a stable foreign exchange value for the Deutschmark as a secondary goal. Price stability is taken to mean a near-zero increase – at most, 2 per cent when there are ameliorating conditions – in the price level.

The Bundesbank regards inflation as a monetary phenomenon in the medium term, and therefore its commitment to price stability translates into a policy of monetary targeting. The view that inflation can be determined by controlling the growth of the money stock is consistent with the Bundesbank Act and the convictions of German central bankers. The Bundesbank adopted and published a monetary target for the first time in December 1974 and, although the target has been formulated in different ways over time, it has kept a target ever since.

The Bundesbank bases its annual money growth target in large part on the growth in potential real output and the unavoidable increase in the price level. If the demand for money is stable, then the non-inflationary percentage change in the money stock is identically equal to the sum of the percentage changes in potentially real output and the price level. For example, the Bundesbank based its 3–6 per cent target range for 1988 on a 2.5 per cent increase in potential real output and a 2 per cent increase in the price level.[1] The sum of these two projected growth rates equals the 4.5 per cent midpoint of the 1988 money growth target range.

The Bundesbank's commitment to a stable foreign exchange value for the Deutschmark has also influenced monetary policy. As the Mundell-Fleming model of an open economy in a regime of fixed exchange rates and capital mobility suggests, a central bank's formal and informal exchange rate commitments constrain monetary policy. The appreciation of the US dollar in 1983–5 led the Bundesbank to sell dollars in the foreign exchange market, and thus tighten monetary policy. The expansion of the money supply slowed from 8 per cent in the first quarter of 1983 to 4 per cent in the second quarter of 1985. When the US dollar fell in 1985, the Bundesbank bought dollars and thus pursued a looser monetary policy. In 1986–8, because falling oil prices and the collapsing dollar restrained inflation, the exchange commitments under the Louvre Accord were allowed to lead to a monetary expansion in excess of target.

Similarly, the commitment to fixed exchange rates in the EMS has influenced monetary policy. Interventions in support of other EMS currencies have had expansionary effects on monetary policy. In January 1987, under the pressure of large capital inflows, the Bundesbank finally agreed to a cut in interest rates. Interest rates were reduced again in November 1987 for similar reasons.

In the Netherlands the key objectives of monetary policy are balance and stability. This is interpreted to mean maintaining the internal and external value of the currency. The connection between the two is, of course, the inflation rate. Thus, monetary policy in the Netherlands aims, first and foremost, to hold the domestic inflation rate no higher than that prevailing in Germany, its major trading partner.

In this sense, Dutch monetary policy has both a single purpose and clear target, which the other countries of our study lack. Domestic price stability is felt to be the key to export competitiveness. Thus the EMS provides an international framework that is fully consistent with its domestic objectives. Although as a trading nation the Netherlands looks beyond Europe, in the absence of a wider international system of exchange rate stability the EMS provides an important and well-accepted anchor for monetary policy.

In France, the objective of monetary policy has undergone a significant shift from promoting growth to controlling inflation. Arguably, this shift began in 1977, when the *Banque de France* published a target for the growth of a broad money aggregate (M2) for the first time. Until the inflationary experience of the 1970s supported the view that inflation is a monetary phenomenon in the medium term, inflation had been regarded as a cost-push phenomenon, to be dealt with by a prices and incomes policy.

In the highly regulated financial environment of the 1970s, monetary policy pursued multiple objectives. The monetary authorities sought to defend the exchange rate by influencing interest rates in the money market, to promote investment by controlling interest rates in the bond market, and to contain inflation by imposing credit ceilings. The *Banque de France* could separate control of the money supply from its interest rate policy because capital controls prevented private borrowers from raising funds abroad and the narrow domestic capital market forced private borrowers to turn to the banking system for their financing needs.

From 1977 to 1980 and since 1983, monetary policy in France has been oriented explicitly towards controlling inflation. In the latter period, rather than stressing monetary targets, the *Banque de France* has emphasized its commitment to the EMS. This was thought to be an effective anti-inflationary policy because of the combination of two factors: the mechanism of adjustment in the EMS and the Bundesbank's low-inflation policy. If two countries fix their common exchange rate and pursue different monetary policies, eventually reserve losses will force the country pursuing the more expansionary policy either to abandon the fixed exchange rate or to tighten monetary policy. As long as the exchange rate remained fixed, the adjustment mechanism implied that the course of monetary policy in France would be similar to that in Germany. In fact, the rate of money growth declined substantially after 1984.

In Britain, as in France, the objectives of monetary policy have changed dramatically. For most of the 1970s, monetary policy was the junior partner in a framework of Keynesian demand management which sought to minimize the level of unemployment. Fiscal policy was given the primary responsibility in fine-tuning the economy, while monetary policy (with the help of credit controls) was directed at achieving low interest rates. As in France during this period, inflation was regarded as a cost-push phenomenon, to be kept under control by a prices and incomes policy.

Mrs Thatcher's electoral victory in 1979 marked an important change in the objectives of economic policy in general and of monetary policy in particular. According to the new thinking at the Treasury, the experience of the 1970s suggested several important lessons: (1) high and variable inflation constrained growth; (2) a prices and incomes policy failed to control inflation and distorted microeconomic incentives; and (3) a credible anti-inflation policy required control of the money stock and the government budget deficit.

The objective of the medium-term financial strategy (MTFS), introduced with the budget of March 1980, was 'to bring down the rate of inflation and to create the conditions for a sustainable growth of output and employment'. The change in objectives was summarized by Nigel Lawson: prior to 1979, macroeconomic policy was directed at promoting growth and employment, and microeconomic policy was supposed to control inflation, while after 1979 their roles were reversed.[2]

Just how far the new objective of low inflation was supported by a new view of the inflationary process is a matter of debate. Certainly, interest rates were seen as crucial in determining the level of demand in the economy, and therefore in influencing inflation. In order to focus on domestic economic policy, the government decided to keep sterling outside the exchange rate mechanism (ERM) of the EMS, and allowed the exchange rate to float freely. Further, the government eschewed fine-tuning and emphasized the medium term.

In order to reduce inflation as quickly and painlessly as possible, the government announced its targets for monetary growth, so that economic agents could anticipate the tight money policy. As part of the MTFS, the government announced targets for the growth of a broad money aggregate, £M3, which consists of currency in circulation and all British private-sector sterling deposits held in British banks. The £M3 target allowed the government's fiscal and monetary targets to be projected on a consistent basis, and according to econometric evidence the demand for £M3 was at least as stable as that for other aggregates. Nevertheless, between 1980 and 1982, the growth of £M3 regularly overshot its targets; however, virtually every other indicator was consistent with a policy of tight money.

After 1983 there seems to have been another change in the government's economic objectives. Having reduced inflation steadily to under 5 per cent in 1983, the government declared in the 1984 budget that its 'ultimate objective' was 'stable prices with lower interest rates', but no timetable was set for achieving this objective. In fact, the targets for the growth of monetary aggregates continued to be overshot, and inflation showed no tendency to fall much below 5 per cent. When inflation rose above this figure, as in 1985 and 1988–9, the government was prepared to raise short-term interest rates substantially. The experience suggests that, providing inflation did not exceed 5 per cent, the government gave priority to growth. The yield on long-term bonds indicates that the financial markets reached the same verdict.

The change in the objectives of monetary policy was accompanied by the *de facto* abandonment of monetary targeting in 1985. The exchange rate began to assume more importance as an intermediate target, and for a period in 1987–8 the government appeared to be closely shadowing the Deutschmark. This broke down when inflation seemed to be accelerating and the Prime Minister was reluctant to see interest rates drop to keep the pound from rising. The controversy over the influence of the exchange rate on domestic monetary conditions intensified during 1989, culminating in the resignation of the Chancellor of the Exchequer.

In sum, while the German monetary authorities have always emphasized low inflation, and the Dutch have wholeheartedly latched themselves on to the German coat-tails, the monetary authorities in France and Britain have less consistent histories. Since 1983, the French authorities have been committed to an anti-inflation policy, which is widely regarded as successful. But in the UK, after a tough anti-inflation stance in the early 1980s, the government seems to have reverted to a stop/go policy by reinstating growth as the primary objective, subject to an inflation ceiling of 5 per cent. Hence, although there has been a general convergence in monetary policy objectives, some governments have not yet stuck to anti-inflation policies doggedly enough for long enough to gain market credibility. It is clear that EMU requires convergence in the monetary policy objectives of all member countries with respect to inflation. As long as Germany firmly sticks to an objective of near-zero inflation, the implementation of EMU hinges on other countries accepting the German lead and the discipline it entails.

Monetary policy implementation: institutional issues

In addition to a European monetary policy directed towards price stability, the German government insists that a European central bank must be independent of national and supra-national governments. Like price stability, the goal of central bank independence is rooted in the two periods of hyperinflation in Germany. These periods of chronic inflation were due in part to the German government's use of the central bank to finance the two world wars. These experiences have led to a national desire for a central bank independent of the government.

The German Bundesbank is legally independent of the government. Although the Bundesbank is required to support the economic policies of the federal government, the Bundesbank Act (Section 12) states explicitly that this obligation must not interfere with the primary objective of monetary policy, which is price stability. At the same time, there are rules to foster consultation and cooperation between the Bundesbank and the federal government. For example, members of the federal government have the right to attend meetings of the Central Bank Council, where they have no vote, but may propose motions and request the deferral of a decision for up to two weeks. The same kind of procedure applies to the attendance of the Bundesbank at discussions of the Financial Planning Council.

The independence of the Netherlands' central bank is guaranteed by the Bank Law of 1948 which nationalized it to make the state the only shareholder. The members of its policy-making body are appointed for seven-year terms, which is longer than any government can expect to remain in power. The Bank Law specifies that the Bank's primary function is to maintain price stability; i.e. the domestic and external purchasing power of the guilder. In order to do so, the Bank is empowered to regulate the money supply and intervene in the exchange markets, although a realignment of exchange rates is in the province of the finance minister.

By contrast, the central banks in France and Britain are not independent of their respective governments. In France, the *Banque de France* functions as an arm of the Treasury. The governor of the *Banque* is appointed by the government and may be dismissed at will.

Similarly, in Britain, the autonomy of the Bank of England is very limited. In principle, the Bank, as a public corporation, manages its own affairs. However, it is governed by a Court of Directors, all of whom are appointed by the Prime Minister. Traditionally, the governor of the Bank was appointed with the tacit approval of the leader of the opposition, on the understanding that the governor would not be replaced when the government changed. However, the present governor, Mr Leigh-Pemberton, was appointed without such consultation and might well be asked to resign if the government changes before the end of his term. At one time, the Bank could determine monetary policy independently of the Treasury, but today it would not undertake a major policy initiative without the full support of the government. By now, monetary policy has become fully integrated into the government's general economic strategy.

Although there are significant differences in the degrees of independence of the central banks in Germany and the Netherlands on the one hand, and France and Britain on the other, the lack of independence *per se* of national central banks need not be an insurmountable obstacle to monetary union.

What matters is the method of decision-making within any European central bank and the restrictions on budget deficit financing by that central bank. As could be expected, the national central bank governors on the Delors committee expressed their preference for an independent central bank, but governments have not yet come to grips with the legal and political implications of this objective. Sorting those out would be the most important task in Stage 2 of the Delors committee process.

Monetary policy implementation: instruments

In Germany, the instruments of monetary policy include reserve requirements, discount lending, open-market operations and public-sector deposits. The Bundesbank requires banks to hold a minimum level of reserves against deposits; these minimum reserve requirements may be changed and have at times been used as a tool of monetary policy. Second, the Bundesbank can determine the price and quantity of central bank credit, which consists of discount credit and Lombard credit. Third, the Bundesbank can engage in open-market operations in the money market and the foreign exchange market. In the money market, the Bundesbank may sell Treasury bills and make repurchase agreements in commercial bills and securities. In the foreign exchange market, the Bundesbank may make exchange rate swaps and engage in repurchase operations. Finally, the Bundesbank can influence liquidity by moving public-sector deposits into the banking system. The Bundesbank is prohibited from limiting the amount of credit granted to non-banks and imposing ceilings on interest rates in the credit or bond markets.

Stability of exchange rates in the Netherlands is pursued through intervention in the money market and through changes in short-term interest rates. The latter is most often pursued through open-market transactions, but changes in the discount rate or in reserve requirements are also possible. With these instruments dedicated to the exchange rate, the Dutch central bank has also used credit ceilings to influence the growth of the domestic money supply. Their effectiveness has declined with the integration of financial markets, so recently the Bank has tried to use government bond sales and purchases and the so-called cash-reserve requirement for private banks for this purpose.

Since the late 1970s, the financial system in France has changed dramatically. In 1978 the Monory Act promoted the development of the stock market, and since 1980 various regulatory changes have encouraged strong growth in the bond market. In 1984 the Banking Act introduced universal banking, i.e. prudential regulations apply to all credit institutions and new financial instruments may be offered by any credit institution. In 1986 markets for commercial paper and negotiable Treasury bills were launched. Interest rates, commissions and fees have all been deregulated. Exchange controls on firms and financial institutions have been lifted (though restrictions on the retail market remain in force until 1 July 1990).

As a result, the instruments of monetary policy have changed from quantitative restrictions on credit to market-based operating procedures. From 1985 to 1986 a transitional scheme, in which progressive reserve requirements on bank credit replaced the credit ceilings, was in operation. At the end of 1986 compulsory reserves on credit were lifted, and an interest rate policy was implemented. Today, reserve requirements are low and stable,[3] and are not regarded as an important tool of monetary policy in the short run. The *Banque de France* controls the two leading rates in the money market: the interest rate on bids by the central bank and the rate on 5–10 day repurchase agreements with the central bank. The actual interbank rate is generally between these two rates. Since the secondary market for Treasury bills is thin, the central bank has so far refrained from pursuing an active open-market policy. Today the *Banque de France* controls the supply of central bank money by manipulating short-term interest rates.

As in France, the financial system in Britain has been deregulated over the past decade. The instruments of monetary policy have changed from quantitative controls to market-based mechanisms: in 1979 exchange controls were abolished; in 1980 quantitative restrictions on the expansion of deposits, known as the 'corset', were eliminated; and in 1982 all hire-purchase controls were removed. Since banks are not required to hold a minimum level of reserves against deposits, the Bank of England's only instruments are short-term interest rates and interventions in the foreign exchange market.

Inevitably there are differences in the monetary instruments used by these countries. Nevertheless, the differences have narrowed over time and there are some important similarities –

for example, the instruments are nearly all price- rather than quantity-related. It is unlikely that remaining differences will by themselves impede progress towards monetary union, though they will obviously have an important bearing on how any European central bank operates.

Political objectives and attitudes towards EMU

It is clear from earlier chapters that the process of European economic integration will not, by itself, bring about monetary union. A political leap will be required, and this is where the difficult issues of sovereignty arise. These can be overcome only if each government sees that it can achieve other political aims through EMU. It is natural for these aims to differ among countries. Such differences need not block the road to EMU, but they will shape the internal debate and thus the inter-country negotiations.

In Germany, the current debate about monetary union is not unlike the pan-European debate of the early 1970s. In the earlier discussions, the 'monetarists' saw monetary union as the driving force behind economic and political integration (Jacques Rueff, 'L'Europe se fera par la monnaie, ou ne se fera pas.'), while the 'economists' held that monetary union could be introduced only when the preconditions for a single currency (i.e. full harmonization of economic policies) had been achieved. Today certain members of the government, and virtually the entire opposition, are taking a distinctly monetarist view. In an attempt to use the symbol of a common currency to promote European unification, the Foreign Minister, Hans-Dietrich Genscher, supports the early establishment of a European central bank.

On the other hand, the Bundesbank and the Council of Experts to the Ministry for Economic Affairs (CEMEA) argue that a greater convergence of policies and performances must be achieved before monetary union is established. H. Schlesinger, the vice-president of the Bundesbank, has supported parallel movements towards economic and monetary union, and opposed using monetary union as an instrument of economic union. The Bundesbank considers the substantial differences in inflation rates and budget deficits between the EC countries to be impediments to uniform interest and exchange rates. Since monetary union involves the irrevocable fixing of parities (or a single currency), nominal exchange rate changes are no longer available to relieve intra-union tensions caused by changes in productivity or other shocks. Therefore, intra-union adjustments must be accomplished by changes in prices, and especially in wages. In the opinion of the Bundesbank, wage determination in the member countries of the EC is not sufficiently flexible to achieve such adjustments.

According to the Bundesbank, the next step towards monetary union are the completion of the single market in the EC (so that the integrated financial market will increase pressures for policy convergence), participation of all EC countries in the exchange rate mechanism (ERM) of the EMS, greater independence for those central banks that are under the control of the government, greater emphasis on price stability in the economic policies of various EC countries, and greater convergence in economic performance.

Along similar lines, the CEMEA sees an increase in the asymmetry of adjustment in the EMS as a step towards monetary union. The argument is that the low rate of monetary growth that will one day be determined by the European central bank must in the mean time come from one or more of the stability-conscious national central banks (i.e. the Bundesbank). The Bundesbank's low rate of money growth can only be made effective by the asymmetrical adjustment requirement, which is enforced by limiting the intervention potential of the less stability-conscious central banks. Therefore, the CEMEA is against measures, such as expanded credit facilities, that relieve the deficit country's burden of adjustment.

Germany's position on progression toward EMU is firmly risk averse. Only when other countries have absorbed the attitudes and conditions that it considers essential for price stability, and when the institutional framework and safeguards are in place to enforce compliance, is it ready to proceed.

The Netherlands' position on the Delors Report and EMU is very close to that of the Germans. Both the government and the Dutch Central Bank have stated that further convergence of economic and monetary policy among the EC member states is a prerequisite to institutional steps such as the creation of a European central bank. Although inflation rates have converged, important differences remain in budget deficits and the level of official debt. These differences will not be corrected by institutional initiatives. Work on that should begin only when it is demonstrated that the present EMS/ERM can cope with the entry of high-inflation countries and the free movement of capital.

In France, monetary integration is seen as a fundamental step in the overall process of European integration, including political integration. Thus progress towards monetary union is supported in order to participate in the decision-making process of monetary policy in Europe, to capture the benefits of a single currency, and to satisfy the exigencies of the 1992 process. Besides, the French have a long tradition of promoting fixed exchange rates.

Monetary union is considered an important tool in creating a more united EC, which would be able to play a greater role on the world stage. The degree of policy coordination required to support a single monetary policy and the symbolic importance of a single currency are seen as important forces behind economic and political integration. The economic power of a united EC would be able to rival that of the United States or Japan, so that the EC, and France, would have a greater say in global affairs.

Second, monetary integration is seen as a way to participate in the decision-making process that ultimately constrains French monetary policy. Since France emphasizes the commitment to a fixed exchange rate with Germany and the burden of adjustment in the EMS falls mostly on the deficit country, monetary policy in France is constrained to be similar to that in Germany. This characteristic of the adjustment mechanism in the EMS is referred to as the 'asymmetry' problem. In a monetary union, the cooperative setting of policy in an institutional framework would give France a greater say than it has now.

In view of this goal of greater participation in the decision-making process, France has supported greater policy coordination and other moves to mitigate the asymmetry in the EMS. In the opinion of the French authorities, the Nyborg Agreement of September 1987 was a step in the right direction, albeit a small one. The Nyborg Agreement created new credit facilities to finance interventions and split the burden of intramarginal interventions between the deficit country and the surplus country. The French authorities point to the coordinated interest rate response to the November 1987 exchange rate crisis as a good illustration of the Nyborg Agreement in action. In January 1988 a joint Franco–German economic and financial council was established to improve the various aspects of policy coordination.

Third, the French government places considerable weight on the benefits of a single currency in the EC. At present, despite similar inflation rates in France and Germany and the French government's commitment to follow the Deutschmark in any realignment, interest rates in France are consistently above those in Germany. The French government is gradually succeeding in restoring credibility in its economic policy, thus slowly but significantly driving down the interest differential with Germany. But it is a long and hard process to regain lost credibility. Despite the government's statements to the contrary, the financial markets do not yet rule out an eventual devaluation of the French franc. With a single currency, no changes in exchange rates would be possible, so risk-adjusted interest rates would be the same throughout the monetary union.

Finally, the 1992 process is believed to make a single currency in the EC strongly desirable. The French fear that the removal of capital controls may threaten the viability of the EMS. The French government takes this threat very seriously, but being strongly committed to financial liberalization believes that the only way to preserve the benefits of fixed exchange rates is to proceed to monetary union. Also, the French government sees a single currency as necessary to capture the full benefits of the 1992 process.

In Britain, the issue of monetary union is dominated by the question of sterling participation in the exchange rate mechanism of the EMS. The main argument in favour is that a tight link between sterling and the Deutschmark would provide an anchor for inflation. Participation in the ERM is also expected to reduce the volatility of sterling and the possibility of misalignments, lower nominal interest rates by reducing the risk premium, and enhance Britain's position in the EC.

At the Madrid Summit of EC heads of government, the British Prime Minister softened her longstanding opposition and committed herself to eventual sterling participation in the ERM. She accepted the plan to embark on Stage 1 of the Delors Report in June 1990. At the same time, Mrs Thatcher listed three conditions for sterling entry into the ERM: (1) British inflation must be significantly lower (in June 1989 it was 8.3 per cent); (2) the remaining capital controls in the EC must be removed; and (3) real progress towards the completion of the single market must be achieved, including free trade in services and a stronger competition policy. These conditions are sensible ones, but not unambiguous. They mark a step towards ERM participation by Britain, but leave plenty of negotiating room. Depending on how strictly these conditions are interpreted, sterling participation in the ERM may yet be considerably delayed.

Beyond the question of sterling and the ERM, the official attitude to EMU – shared by both Treasury and Bank of England officials – is one of scepticism. There is a strong feeling that premature and utopian moves to monetary union (for example early adoption of a common currency) must be avoided. The accent is on letting the single-market programme make the running, with progress towards monetary union following at a cautious and evolutionary pace. It should be added that whereas the government has been criticized within the UK for not taking sterling into the ERM earlier, there has been very little domestic criticism of its sceptical attitude to EMU. The current British government is unlikely to commit itself to anything like Stages 2 and 3 of the Delors Report.

In sum, the German, Dutch, French and British governments have substantially different views on monetary union. France stresses the benefits of monetary union; Germany and the Netherlands are more even-handed; and in Britain there is very little interest in anything beyond putting sterling into the ERM, which itself is not certain. Although three of the four governments support full monetary integration, the longstanding debate between the economists and the monetarists has not been resolved. The German and Dutch authorities favour a greater convergence of economic policies and performances before moving to monetary union, while the French want to use monetary union as a vehicle for economic integration. Further, the opposing German/Dutch and French views on the asymmetry phenomenon make incremental progress difficult. While France is a supporter of greater symmetry in the EMS, the Bundesbank and the CEMEA in Germany are adamantly opposed to any such moves. Indeed, if it were not for Mrs Thatcher's objections to monetary union, the differences between the German and the French positions might be far more striking.

Prospects for monetary union

The EC is still a long way from monetary union. Yet those members whose currencies adhere to the narrow margin arrangements of the ERM already experience many of its

benefits – and costs. The 1992 process will affect the balance of
these benefits and costs for countries outside the ERM, and the
marginal gains to be achieved – or past gains put at risk – by full
ERM members considering the prospects of EMU.

In many respects, the Dutch experience holds the most
interesting lessons for the other countries. As economic
integration proceeded with the rest of the EC, and especially
with Germany, the case for a firmer monetary linkage to the
Deutschmark became progressively stronger. When financial
instability worsened outside Europe with the excessive rise of
the US dollar in the early 1980s, the benefits of greater
exchange rate stability through closer EC ties were increased.
At the same time, support was generated on the home front by
the lower domestic inflation and stable export competitiveness
that the DM link brought. By now the Dutch authorities and,
indeed, the general public see Holland's EMS/ERM obligations
as the tool to achieve European, international and domestic
objectives. It is widely perceived that, whatever the costs may
be, there is no alternative. Yet there is also a reluctance to move
rapidly toward EMU. Incremental benefits appear small
compared to the risk to the entire EMS structure should it try to
lock in higher-inflation countries too soon.

No doubt the Dutch embrace of close monetary cooperation is
partly conditioned by the small size of its economy. In that
respect it cannot be directly generalized to the case of France or
the UK. Nonetheless, it illustrates well how EMS could evolve
into EMU with few institutional initiatives. The balancing of
EMS gains against EMU risks boils down to the differing
economic and political objectives for EMU. From a strictly
economic point of view, the low-inflation core of the area –
Germany, Holland, Austria and Switzerland – could probably
move ahead now to a coordinating central bank and perhaps
even a common currency, thereby achieving the benefits of full
EMU without much risk of a transitional rupture caused by
international market reaction or domestic political opposition.
But such a move, involving two non-EC countries and only two
of the twelve EC member states would be contrary to the
political aims of the European Community and, for that reason,
also out of the question for Germany and Holland.

If the political objective of a single money for a single market
is to be achieved, then the process toward EMU must
accommodate all EC members. This will naturally slow it down.
However, it need not constrain all countries to move at the pace

of the slowest, as the Delors Report implies. The divisions between stages could be constructed as milestones that countries pass as they are ready rather than as chronological dates which all countries must pass together.

The EMS itself provides a good example of the milestone approach. Portugal is not yet a member, the UK and Greece do not participate in the ERM, Spain and Italy have wider margins of fluctuation for their currencies within the ERM, while the other seven countries of the EC have committed themselves to a tighter ERM linkage.

The diversity that still remains in the objectives and implementation of monetary policy across Europe does not bode well for rapid movement along the Delors Report path toward European monetary union. We believe that both the speed of movement and the prospects for reaching that eventual aim would be increased by a process that could accommodate a range of participation levels along the way. The internal momentum of the process would be maintained by matching the involvement in joint decision-making with the degree of commitment to joint aims over national ones.

Such a process would not, in our view, lead to a two-speed Europe. It would recognize that the member states of the EC are already moving at twelve different speeds. Harnessing them into an eventual monetary union may be easier by allowing the core that has already formed to add members one by one or two by two, as the ERM has done, than by asking all potential members to sign on for the entire process before embarking on the first stretch.

Unless a more flexible approach is adopted, we do not think the probability of EMU by the mid-1990s is very high. If the political priority given to EMU remains low in two or more of the larger member states, then little further movement can be expected. If, after the 1992 programme is largely complete, the political momentum shifts on to EMU, then there is a significant risk that institutional developments will be overwhelmed by the extra strain imposed by higher-inflation countries.

There is, in addition to the economic and political developments in the EC, an important interplay of European with wider international and domestic factors that will influence progress toward EMU. As an example of the latter, a post-Thatcher government in the UK, of whichever party, is likely to be more pro-Europe than the current regime. On the other hand, the rapid move toward economic and monetary union between the two Germanys and the many problems which must be solved in that context may crowd EMU off the political agenda for German policy-makers.

At the international level, it is important to remember that the impressive degree of agreement on anti-inflation objectives among EMS members has been achieved against a benign global economic background of low inflation and sustained growth. It remains to be seen whether such consensus will be maintained if we face rising unemployment and moderate inflation, especially if there were a swing to the left on the political spectrum.

All this illustrates the complex interdependence of progress towards a single market and progress towards monetary union. If the 1992 process does enhance growth prospects this could reduce the likelihood of macroeconomic policy U-turns and divergencies. It could also facilitate a united response to changes in Eastern Europe. But the essential problem remains. Economic union is a process that can be facilitated by monetary union, but monetary union is a state that cannot be achieved and maintained without a high degree of economic union among its members.

Notes

1. *Monthly Report of the Deutsche Bundesbank*, January 1987.
2. June 1984, Mais lecture.
3. Since May 1989, reserve requirements have been 5% on demand deposits, and 2.5% on time deposits, savings accounts, and related financial instruments.

Index